AMERICA'S VOLUNTEER MILITARY

STUDIES IN DEFENSE POLICY

AMERICA'S VOLUNTEER MILITARY:
PROGRESS AND PROSPECTS

Martin Binkin

THE BROOKINGS INSTITUTION
Washington, D.C.

Library of Congress Cataloging in Publication data:

Binkin, Martin, 1928–
  America's volunteer military.
  (Studies in defense policy)
  Includes bibliographical references.
  1. Military service, Voluntary—United States.
2. United States—Armed Forces. I. Title. II. Series.
UB323.B565 1984   355.2′2363′0973   84-14943
ISBN 0-8157-0975-7 (pbk.)

9 8 7 6 5 4 3 2 1

THE BROOKINGS INSTITUTION is an independent organization devoted to nonpartisan research, education, and publication in economics, government, foreign policy, and the social sciences generally. Its principal purposes are to aid in the development of sound public policies and to promote public understanding of issues of national importance.

The Institution was founded on December 8, 1927, to merge the activities of the Institute for Government Research, founded in 1916, the Institute of Economics, founded in 1922, and the Robert Brookings Graduate School of Economics and Government, founded in 1924.

The Board of Trustees is responsible for the general administration of the Institution, while the immediate direction of the policies, program, and staff is vested in the President, assisted by an advisory committee of the officers and staff. The by-laws of the Institution state: "It is the function of the Trustees to make possible the conduct of scientific research, and publication, under the most favorable conditions, and to safeguard the independence of the research staff in the pursuit of their studies and in the publication of the results of such studies. It is not a part of their function to determine, control, or influence the conduct of particular investigations or the conclusions reached."

The President bears final responsibility for the decision to publish a manuscript as a Brookings book. In reaching his judgment on the competence, accuracy, and objectivity of each study, the President is advised by the director of the appropriate research program and weighs the views of a panel of expert outside readers who report to him in confidence on the quality of the work. Publication of a work signifies that it is deemed a competent treatment worthy of public consideration but does not imply endorsement of conclusions or recommendations.

The Institution maintains its position of neutrality on issues of public policy in order to safeguard the intellectual freedom of the staff. Hence interpretations or conclusions in Brookings publications should be understood to be solely those of the authors and should not be attributed to the Institution, to its trustees, officers, or other staff members, or to the organizations that support its research.

FOREWORD

WITH the decision to abolish military conscription in 1973, the United States took on a monumental task: raising an armed force of 3 million by strictly voluntary means. A key concern was whether the services could enlist enough young men and women without incurring exorbitant additional costs and without compromising the quality and therefore the effectiveness of the armed forces.

Despite several threatening developments in the late 1970s, the all-volunteer force survived the decade; and during the early 1980s the military services enjoyed unparalleled success in recruiting qualified volunteers. Thus many proponents contend that the peacetime volunteer military has now earned its place as a permanent institution in American society. However, opponents of voluntary recruitment maintain that it conflicts with the democratic ideal of civic duty or that it is inequitable and inefficient. But these criticisms in themselves are unlikely to promote public debate of this politically charged issue.

The greater threat to the volunteer system lies in the potential convergence of demographic, economic, and technological trends, each of which could adversely affect the armed forces' ability to attract and retain enough qualified personnel over the next decade.

In this study Martin Binkin reviews how the nation fared in manning the armed forces with volunteers in the first ten years following the end of conscription. He also assesses the prospects for maintaining the volunteer system, taking into account the upcoming decline in the youth population, anticipated increases in the complexity of military weapons, and possible changes in the economy.

The author concludes that despite recent successes the volunteer concept is not assured of survival: the armed forces will have to settle for fewer or less capable recruits as competition intensifies with civilian employers and higher education institutions for the shrinking number of young Americans. But he discounts the prospects for a return to peacetime conscription, unless there are substantial increases in military strength requirements and entrance standards or in college participation rates. Should these happen, the practical options available to deal with military manpower deficiencies on a voluntary basis could fall short and the conscription issue would reappear on the national agenda.

Martin Binkin, a senior fellow in the Brookings Foreign Policy Studies program, is author or coauthor of ten previous books in the series of Brookings Studies in Defense Policy. He is grateful to Richard Danzig and General Edward C. Meyer (U.S. Army, retired), as well as Daniel Huck and Charles C. Moskos, for helpful comments on the manuscript. He is also indebted to Kenneth Scheflen and his staff at the Defense Manpower Data Center and to W. Vance Grant of the National Center for Educational Statistics for their assistance.

The author also thanks John D. Steinbruner, director of the Foreign Policy Studies program, and David W. Breneman, a former Brookings colleague, for valuable suggestions; Nancy D. Davidson for editing the manuscript; Carolyn A. Rutsch for verifying its factual content; and Ann M. Ziegler for patiently and skillfully processing the manuscript.

The study was financed by a grant from the Andrew W. Mellon Foundation, whose assistance the Brookings Institution gratefully acknowledges. The views expressed are those of the author and should not be ascribed to the Mellon Foundation, to those who commented on the manuscript, or to the trustees, officers, or other staff members of the Brookings Institution.

BRUCE K. MACLAURY
President

May 1984
Washington, D.C.

AMERICA'S VOLUNTEER MILITARY: PROGRESS AND PROSPECTS

THE abandonment of conscription in 1973 was a highly controversial step at the time, and the procurement of military manpower by strictly voluntary means has been a contentious national policy ever since. Questions have been raised repeatedly about its efficiency, effectiveness, and equitability.

Doubts about the feasibility of the concept were strongest in the late 1970s, when recruitment and retention of qualified volunteers began to experience serious problems. The extent of and the reasons for the setbacks remain matters of speculation, but several factors are believed to have contributed: military pay raises lagged behind private-sector increases; educational benefits for members of the armed forces were reduced while student aid for civilians was increased; and recruiting and advertising budgets did not keep pace with inflation. In addition, the armed forces' public image, barely recovered from the Vietnam experience, was tarnished by the *Mayaguez* incident and the Iranian hostage crisis.

The unfavorable manning trends bottomed out at the turn of the decade, however, and both recruitment and retention have improved in the early 1980s. The reversal can be attributed to several factors: military pay was raised by roughly one-third as a result of increases granted in 1980 and 1981; the unemployment rolls grew as the recession deepened; educational benefits for military recruits were improved while student aid programs were targeted for cuts; more resources were allocated to recruiting; and there were signs that the American public, perhaps aroused by the patriotic theme of the Reagan administration, once again supported the country's military institutions.

These favorable developments might appear to have settled the issue, but there are good reasons to ask whether the successes of the early

1

1980s can be sustained, given the prospect that the military could run up against an adverse supply-and-demand situation later in the decade. On the supply side, not only will the pool of qualified youth shrink as the baby-boom generation passes beyond military age, but anticipated economic recovery could cause fewer young people to be interested in the military. Meanwhile, on the demand side, should proposed increases in the size of the armed forces and expected advances in weapons technology materialize, the military may have to attract not only more recruits, but better ones.

If these events happen, there are a variety of practical options open to decisionmakers to modify the demand for, or increase the supply of, qualified volunteers: job opportunities for women could be expanded; civilians could be substituted for military personnel in appropriate occupations; volunteers could be encouraged to serve longer periods; and new recruitment markets (community colleges, for example) could be opened. There is wide disagreement over how far these changes could be pushed without undermining military effectiveness. Moreover, since these measures run counter to deeply rooted traditions, the armed services cannot be counted upon to pursue them vigorously. For these reasons, it is more likely that future manning problems will be met with calls for additional financial incentives and, should these fail, a reinstitution of conscription.

The purpose here is to review the progress of the nation's volunteer military in the first decade following the end of conscription and to assess its prospects for the next.

Taking Stock: The First Decade

Whether the volunteers manning the U.S. armed forces have been up to the task of protecting national interests has been at issue since the end of the draft. Heading the list of concerns have been the diminished size of the armed forces, the low caliber of their recruits, the heavy losses of experienced technicians and specialists, shortages in reserve manning levels, overrepresentation of minorities (particularly in the ground combat forces), and a perceived deterioration of unit cohesiveness.

Military Strength

In 1973, when the president's draft authority expired, total American active-duty military strength numbered just over 2.25 million. Already

Table 1. Military Personnel Strengths, by Service, End of Selected Fiscal Years, 1950–83

Thousands

	Service				
Year	Army	Navy	Marine Corps	Air Force	Total
1950[a]	593	382	74	411	1,460
1952[b]	1,669	810	243	953	3,675
1960	868	612	171	814	2,465
1968[c]	1,570	765	307	905	3,548
1973[d]	801	565	196	691	2,253
1974	783	546	189	644	2,162
1975	784	535	196	613	2,128
1976	783	528	190	583	2,084
1977	782	530	192	571	2,075
1978	772	530	191	570	2,062
1979	759	524	185	559	2,027
1980	777	527	188	558	2,051
1981	781	540	191	570	2,083
1982	780	553	192	583	2,108
1983	780	558	194	592	2,123

Sources: Data through fiscal year 1981, U.S. Department of Defense, *Selected Manpower Statistics, Fiscal Year 1981*, pp. 72–73; fiscal years 1982 and 1983, *Department of Defense Annual Report, Fiscal Year 1985*, p. 284.
a. Before the Korean War.
b. The peak of the Korean War.
c. The peak of the Vietnam War.
d. The last year of the draft.

at its lowest level since 1950, the size of the active forces continued to decrease modestly before reaching a low in 1979 (see table 1). Whether these reductions were somehow justified by technical military assessments or whether, as contended by some critics of voluntary recruitment, the cuts were merely accommodations to a diminished ability to attract volunteers, remains a matter of debate.

There is some evidence that reductions in active-duty military personnel during the period were offset by a growing dependence on contractor-supplied civilians and military reserve units.[1] It is clear, on the other hand, that the small reduction in Army strength in fiscal 1979 was a consequence of its inability to attract enough qualified recruits. But even if the reductions can be attributed to the end of the draft, some proponents of the volunteer concept contend that the nation *should* attune its foreign policy, national security strategy, and military force structure to the costs of military manpower. The value of the volunteer

1. See Martin Binkin, *U.S. Reserve Forces: The Problem of the Weekend Warrior* (Brookings Institution, 1974), p. 8; and Richard V. L. Cooper, *Contract-Hire Personnel in the Department of Defense* (Santa Monica: Rand Corp., 1977).

system, by this argument, is that conscription biases decisions toward using more military personnel than would occur if defense budgets reflected the true marginal costs of manpower.

In any event, attributing the size of the armed forces solely to the method of manpower procurement is overly simplistic; yet it is safe to say that had the nation attempted in the 1970s to maintain pre-Vietnam strength levels, voluntary recruitment would have been an even more tenuous proposition and probably would not have survived the decade. More important, it can be assumed that the unsettling prospect of conscription will have a major influence on future decisions about the size of the U.S. peacetime military establishment.[2]

Recruit Quality

One of the most controversial issues since the end of military conscription has been the "quality" of military manpower: it has been the centerpiece in the recurring debate over the shape of the nation's armed forces. In truth, the concept of quality is elusive; job performance in the military, as in many civilian pursuits, depends on such characteristics as mental ability, educational attainment, job aptitude, physical condition, experience, motivation, adaptability to change, and ability to get along with co-workers. All are interrelated, and their relative importance varies by type of job and experience level within a given occupation.

Individual performance on the job is assessed in several ways. The armed forces have elaborate rating systems in which their members are periodically evaluated by their superiors. A variety of tests are also used; for example, the Army administers a skill qualification test designed to evaluate a soldier's ability to perform job-related tasks. Other criteria include training course grades, disciplinary records, and successful completion of the first enlistment period.

Since the end of the draft, critics of the quality of military volunteers have expressed disappointment with low scores on skill qualification

2. This influence was evident early in the Reagan administration. According to press accounts, the Army indicated in 1981 that "extraordinary manpower policies"—widely interpreted as "conscription"—would be needed if they were to meet higher personnel strengths planned for 1987. (George C. Wilson, "Army Hints Draft May Be Required," *Washington Post*, July 9, 1981.) This proposal, wrote Maj. Gen. Jeanne Holm, "landed on the third floor of the Pentagon with a dull thud. One defense official describes the Secretary's reaction as livid." See Jeanne Holm, *Women in the Military: An Unfinished Revolution* (Presidio Press, 1982), p. 390.

tests, relatively high rates of indiscipline, and an unusually large proportion of volunteers who fail to serve a full first enlistment ("early attrition" in military jargon). Although the question remains open of whether these performance measures are as appropriate as the adherence to them implies, they are widely accepted as barometers of quality. This is important because the armed forces' standards for enlistment, which are defined by educational level and aptitude test score attainment, are rationalized largely on the basis of their validity as predictors of these performance measures. The "choice" recruit, according to the services, has a high school diploma and an above-average aptitude for military skills.

EDUCATIONAL LEVEL. The armed forces place a high premium on the completion of high school, not so much because of its relationship to mental achievement—although that is important for some technical courses—but because of its implications for general adaptability to the military environment. High school dropouts find it difficult to accommodate, attitudinally and emotionally, to the even more demanding military environment. "The significance of a high school diploma," notes one scholar, "is that it reflects the graduate's motivation and ability to accomplish one of society's important goals, to complete one program before beginning another or, in other words, to stick to a project even if the going is difficult."[3] In recent years graduates have been almost twice as likely as dropouts to complete their initial enlistment period. For example, of those male recruits who entered the service in fiscal 1978, 41.4 percent of those who were high school dropouts did not survive the first three years of their enlistment, compared with 22.7 percent of diploma holders, a pattern that has prevailed at least since the end of the draft.[4] These early losses, which increase personnel turbulence and reduce the experience level in military units, are believed to adversely affect group cohesion and effectiveness; they also lead to increased costs since more volunteers must be recruited to maintain a given force size.

The predictive validity of educational attainment has also been pushed

3. Anne Hoiberg, "Meeting Personnel Needs," *Society*, vol. 18 (March–April 1981), p. 39.

4. Derived from data provided by U.S. Department of Defense, Defense Manpower Data Center. The discussion of educational levels and aptitude test scores is partially drawn from Martin Binkin and Mark J. Eitelberg with Alvin J. Schexnider and Marvin M. Smith, *Blacks and the Military* (Brookings Institution, 1982), pp. 86–88.

beyond disciplinary behavior: "In addition to overall military competence, educational achievement has been found to be related to such specific effectiveness criteria as performance in combat and in various military occupational settings."[5] Correlating educational attainment with job performance is tricky, however, not only because of problems in measurement but also because of difficulties in differentiating the effects of education and aptitude.

APTITUDE TEST SCORES. Military aptitude plays an important part in the personnel screening, classification, and assignment process. The services use aptitude scores as the principal predictors of trainability. A standard test, the Armed Services Vocational Aptitude Battery (ASVAB), now administered to all prospective volunteers, is composed of ten subtests: general science, arithmetic reasoning, word knowledge, paragraph comprehension, numerical operations, coding speed, mathematics knowledge, electronics information, mechanical comprehension, and auto and shop information.[6] A composite, which includes word knowledge, arithmetic reasoning, paragraph comprehension, and numerical operations subtests, yields a single index of general trainability, known as the Armed Forces Qualification Test (AFQT) score. On the basis of these test scores, examinees are divided into the following groups representing the range from very high military aptitude (category I) to very low military aptitude (category V):

AFQT category	Percentile score	Net raw score (105 possible)
I	93-100	102-105
II	65-92	84-101
III	31-64	65-83
IV	10-30	38-64
V	9 and below	37 and below

The test scores are used principally to differentiate between categories I and II (above average), III (average), and IV and V (below average). Category III is sometimes divided into two groups, category IIIA (encompassing those who score between the fiftieth and sixty-fourth percentiles) and category IIIB (those who score between the thirty-first

5. Anne Hoiberg, "Military Staying Power," in Sam C. Sarkesian, ed., *Combat Effectiveness: Cohesion, Stress, and the Volunteer Military*, vol. 9 (Sage, 1980), p. 215.

6. For a brief description of the version of the test battery introduced in 1980, see William H. Sims and Ann R. Truss, *Normalization of the Armed Services Vocational Aptitude Battery (ASVAB) Forms 8, 9, and 10 Using a Sample of Service Recruits*, CRC 438 (Arlington, Va.: Center for Naval Analyses, 1980).

and forty-ninth percentiles). Entrants scoring below the thirty-first percentile are considered by the services to require more training and present greater disiplinary problems than those in the higher groups, and those scoring below the tenth percentile are disqualified.[7]

Standardized tests have been administered by the armed forces since World War I. They were used initially to identify the mentally unfit and have been used only more recently to assess vocational aptitude. The services place great stock in the tests, largely because research has shown that individuals with higher aptitude scores are more trainable; that is, they tend to complete skill training courses at a higher rate than low scorers, they complete them sooner, they get higher grades, and they retain the information longer.

QUALITY TRENDS. Changes in the qualitative characteristics of military recruits can be traced with the aid of table 2, which shows educational and aptitude test score attainment for selected periods under both conscription and volunteer conditions.

Enlisted volunteers entering the armed forces since the end of the draft have been less likely than recruits during the draft era to have acquired some college credits but more likely to have a high school diploma; on average, the educational attainment of volunteer-era recruits has not differed appreciably from that of their draft-era predecessors.[8] The relative success in attracting high school graduates is explained in part by the expanded role of women following the end of the draft. The contrast was especially striking in the Army. During fiscal years 1974–76,

7. The percentile ranges of these categories are still defined by the distribution of scores attained by male military personnel (enlisted and officer) during World War II. The categories were set up at the time for "administrative simplicity" according to the following rationale: "In general, the top third, those in Classes I and II, were able to cope with any training program, even the most difficult. Those in the middle third, Class III, could meet most training requirements, other than those that required ability to deal with mathematics and other abstract forms of reasoning. Men in Class IV were expected to absorb basic training and even some of the simpler types of advanced training, but this was not true about the more than 750,000 recruits in Class V. Men in the lowest class were definitely handicapped and could be expected to meet minimum performance standards only if they were given special training, such as a preliminary course to prepare them for basic training, or a prolongation of basic training itself." Eli Ginzberg and others, *The Ineffective Soldier: Lessons for Management and the Nation*, vol. 1: *The Lost Divisions* (Columbia University Press, 1959), p. 45.

8. The large proportion of entrants with college experience during the conscription era can be explained largely by the influence of the draft, while the growing percentage of high school graduates during the volunteer era can be attributed both to a growth in the proportion of young Americans completing high school and to the higher priority placed by the services on attracting graduates.

Table 2. Percentage Distribution of Recruits, by Aptitude Category and Level of Education, All Services, Selected Fiscal Years, 1960–83

Aptitude category and educational level	Draft era			Volunteer era		
	1960–64	*1965–69*	*1970–73*	*1974–76*[a]	*1977–80*[b]	*1981–83*
Armed Forces Qualification Test category						
I and II (above average)	38	38	35	35	29	37
III (average)	49	41	45	55	43	50
IV (below average)	14	21	22	10	28	13
Educational level						
College degree	2	3	5	1	1	2
Some college	11	15	13	5	4	6
High school diploma	51	56	52	60	66	77
Total (having at least high school diploma)	64	74	70	66	71	85

Sources: Fiscal years 1960–69, Richard V. L. Cooper, *Military Manpower and the All-Volunteer Force* (Santa Monica: Rand Corp., 1977), p. 133; fiscal years 1970–73, U.S. Department of Defense, Office of the Assistant Secretary of Defense for Manpower, Reserve Affairs, and Logistics, *America's Volunteers: A Report on the All-Volunteer Armed Forces* (DOD, 1978), pp. 193, 196, 197; author's estimates based on data provided by U.S. Department of Defense, Defense Manpower Data Center, and Office of the Assistant Secretary of Defense for Manpower, Reserve Affairs, and Logistics; fiscal years 1974–83, author's estimates based on data provided by Defense Manpower Data Center.

a. Includes the quarter July–September 1976 to account for the transition to the fiscal year beginning October 1976.

b. Aptitude category data reflect corrections made to misnormed scores as described in text.

for example, of the 53,600 women who enlisted in the Army, close to 47,000 (or 88 percent) had completed high school, while only 52 percent of the male recruits were high school graduates. Thus, while women constituted only 9 percent of all new recruits during the period, they accounted for nearly 15 percent of the total high school graduates. Between fiscal years 1977 and 1980—the most difficult period for the volunteer force—some 68,000 women constituted 12 percent of new Army recruits and accounted for approximately 18 percent of all high school graduates. Finally, the educational differences tended to even out with the recruitment successes of the early 1980s, as the Army was able to attract more male high school graduates. Between 1981 and 1983 women made up 13 percent of Army recruits and accounted for 15 percent of the high school diplomas. Overall, the impact of women on the educational profile of military recruits has been telling: in the decade following the end of the draft, 92 percent of all women who enlisted in the Army had completed high school, compared with just under 62 percent of the men. Had the Army not expanded the opportunities for women soldiers, it is doubtful if the all-volunteer force could have survived the 1970s.[9]

9. The contribution to overall quality that women made in the military services other than the Army was also impressive. Of the women who enlisted in all of the services

Table 3. Percentage Distribution of Army Recruits, by Aptitude Category and Level of Education, Selected Fiscal Years, 1960–83

Aptitude category and educational level	Draft era				Volunteer era		
	1960	1964	1969	1972	1974–76[a]	1977–80[b]	1981–83
Armed Forces Qualification Test category							
I and II (above average)	32	34	35	33	29	18	31
III (average)	51	47	38	49	54	37	49
IV (below average)	17	19	27	18	17	44	20
Educational level							
College degree	5	5	6	4	1	1	2
Some college	26	15	19	11	4	3	6
High school diploma	36	50	45	46	50	58	77
Total (having at least high school diploma)	67	70	70	61	55	62	85

Sources: Fiscal years 1960–72, William K. Brehm, "Peacetime Voluntary Options," in Andrew J. Goodpaster, Lloyd H. Elliott, and J. Allan Hovey, Jr., eds., *Toward a Consensus on Military Service: Report of the Atlantic Council's Working Group on Military Service* (Pergamon, 1982), p. 170; fiscal years 1974–83, author's estimates based on data provided by Defense Manpower Data Center. Figures are rounded.

a. Includes the quarter July–September 1976 to account for the transition to the fiscal year beginning October 1976.

b. Aptitude category data reflect corrections made to misnormed scores as described in text.

The pattern of aptitude test scores since the end of the draft has been irregular. For the first several years, the armed services attracted roughly the same proportion of high-aptitude (category I and II) recruits as they had during the draft years but a substantially larger proportion of those with average aptitude and, commensurately, a smaller percentage of those in the lowest category.[10] The latter part of the 1970s, however, proved to be a difficult time as the effectiveness of the armed forces in general and the quality of their members in particular came under question; in 1977–80, 28 percent of new recruits were in category IV (see table 2). The Army was the most seriously affected; as table 3 reveals, close to half of all its male recruits scored in the bottom category.

This downward shift in the qualifications of new recruits can be partly explained by an improvement in civilian employment opportunities in

over the decade, 92 percent had a high school diploma, compared with about 70 percent of the male recruits. Derived from data provided by the Defense Manpower Data Center.

10. The relatively high proportion of category IV recruits that entered the armed forces during the Vietnam period was a consequence of quotas that were imposed on the services. "Project One Hundred Thousand," intended to rehabilitate the nation's "subterranean poor," was an experimental program for the annual induction of 100,000 men who ordinarily would not qualify for military service. For an analysis of the program see U.S. Department of Defense, Office of the Secretary of Defense, *Project One Hundred Thousand: Characteristics and Performance of "New Standards" Men* (DOD, 1969). These quotas continued in force until the passage of Public Law 92-204 in 1971 prohibited their use (sec. 744, 85 Stat. 735).

the late 1970s, combined with an erosion of financial incentives for prospective military recruits. As highly qualified youths are attracted to better-paying civilian jobs, the armed services are forced to accept more volunteers with lower aptitudes, who generally have fewer opportunities for civilian employment and whose propensity for military service is less affected by relative pay rates. The three principal economic effects are described below.

1. Changes in the ratio of military to civilian pay. The manning problems of the late 1970s, according to one of the principal designers of the volunteer experiment, occurred because the nation reneged on its commitment to maintain competitive levels of pay for service personnel.[11] Military personnel lost ground as a series of pay caps were imposed on federal employees by the Ford and Carter administrations to offset the pressures of inflation. Military pay fell even further behind because it was linked to civilian white-collar pay, which increased less than blue-collar pay over the period. All told, military pay declined by an estimated 10 percent relative to civilian pay between fiscal years 1975 and 1979.[12] On the assumption that a percentage change in the ratio of military to civilian pay yields an equal percentage change in enlistment rates (that is, pay elasticity = 1.0), the relative decline in military pay over the period would have caused a 10 percent decline in the enlistment rates of high-quality male recruits.[13]

2. Changes in youth unemployment. The relative improvement in the nation's economy during the latter part of the 1970s also affected military recruitment. In 1975, when the United States was at the bottom of its deepest recession since 1930, unemployment among male youths aged sixteen to nineteen averaged 18.5 percent. By 1979 the average jobless rate among that group was down to 15.9 percent, a decrease of 14 percent.[14] Analyses of recruitment during the 1970s suggest that a decrease of that magnitude in the youth unemployment rate would be

11. Melvin R. Laird, *People, Not Hardware* (American Enterprise Institute for Public Policy Research, 1980), p. 1.

12. Richard W. Hunter and Gary R. Nelson, "Eight Years with the All-Volunteer Armed Forces: Assessments and Prospects," in Brent Scowcroft, ed., *Military Service in the United States* (Prentice-Hall, 1982), p. 93.

13. Congressional Budget Office, *Costs of Manning the Active-Duty Military*, prepared by Robert F. Hale and Joel N. Slackman (Government Printing Office, 1980), p. 35.

14. Hunter and Nelson, "Eight Years with the All-Volunteer Armed Forces," p. 92.

accompanied by a 3 to 7 percent decrease in enlistments of male high school graduates scoring above the thirtieth percentile on the standardized entry test.[15]

3. Changes in educational benefits. Finally, the demise of the Vietnam-era GI bill and the concurrent expansion of federal assistance to college students are believed to have taken a toll on recruitment. These policy decisions, it has been argued, have created "a system of educational benefits which offers more to those who do not serve their country than to those who do."[16] Effective January 1, 1977, the Vietnam-era GI bill was replaced by the Post-Vietnam Era Veterans' Educational Assistance Program (VEAP), the first contributory military educational benefits bill. Service members who enroll in VEAP voluntarily contribute to an education fund. The maximum contribution is $2,700, which, matched on a two-for-one basis with $5,400 of government funds, provides $8,100 for a veteran's educational expenses. But from the outset the participation rate in VEAP has been disappointing. During the first three years of the program, less than one of every four enlisted personnel opened a VEAP savings account, with the highest rate occurring in the Army (30.2 percent).[17] The conversion of the GI Bill to

15. Estimates of unemployment elasticity generally fall in the range of 0.2 to 0.5. See, for example, Congressional Budget Office, *The Costs of Defense Manpower: Issues for 1977*, prepared by Gary R. Nelson, Robert F. Hale, and Andrew Hamilton (GPO, 1977), p. 135; David W. Grissmer, "The Supply of Enlisted Volunteers in the Post-Draft Environment: An Analysis Based on Monthly Data, 1970-1975," in Richard V. L. Cooper, ed., *Defense Manpower Policy: Presentations from the 1976 Rand Conference on Defense Manpower*, R-2396-ARPA (Santa Monica: Rand Corp., 1979), p. 110; CBO, *Costs of Manning the Active-Duty Military*, p. 38; and Lawrence Goldberg, "Navy Enlisted Supply Study," CNA 81-0601 (Alexandria, Va.: Center for Naval Analyses, 1981).

16. Charles C. Moskos and John H. Faris, "Beyond the Marketplace: National Service and the AVF," in Andrew J. Goodpaster, Lloyd H. Elliott, and J. Allan Hovey, Jr., eds., *Toward a Consensus on Military Service: Report of the Atlantic Council's Working Group on Military Service* (Pergamon, 1982), pp. 131-51.

17. U.S. Department of Defense, Office of the Assistant Secretary of Defense, *Third Annual Report to the Congress on the Post-Vietnam Era Veterans' Educational Assistance Program*, report to the House and Senate Committees on Veterans Affairs (DOD, 1980), pp. 2-6. The participation rates do not account for those who either suspend active participation or drop out of the program entirely. A survey administered in 1979 revealed "considerable movement by eligible enlisted personnel into, out of, and sometimes back into the program." The survey results also suggested that a person's inability to save was the primary reason for dropping out; the program barred or discouraged participation by persons with competing financial responsibilities, and there was "evidence of dissatisfaction with both the administration of the program and the program itself." See Mark J. Eitelberg and John A. Richards, *Survey of Participants*

VEAP, it is estimated, accounted for a decline of between 5 and 10 percent in enlistments of male high school graduates by fiscal year 1979.[18]

Cumulatively, these three factors are said to have accounted for about 80 percent of the decline in the qualitative profile of volunteers during the period.[19] The residual was attributed to "a bad press on problems of the all-volunteer force"; "a low public opinion of military service, buttressed by continued anti-Vietnam sentiment"; "large-scale CETA programs offering jobs to many youths who would otherwise enlist in the military"; and "growing federally-sponsored scholarship programs which make it possible for low and moderate income youth to attend college without a military service commitment."[20]

An additional, but inestimable, share of the problem must be attributed to confusion about entry test results. With the introduction of a new version of the standardized entry test in 1976, errors in converting raw test scores into percentile scores caused the latter to be overstated, with the result that many recruits who would otherwise have been ineligible were accepted by the military services. The magnitude of the error was substantial; for example, in contrast to the original belief that only 5 percent of the recruits who entered the armed forces in fiscal 1979 had scored in category IV, corrected scores placed 30 percent in that category. The Army was the most seriously affected—close to half its recruits were below average rather than 9 percent, as reported originally.[21]

The Pentagon apparently did not know what was happening until 1980. When the problem was finally revealed, a major inconsistency was resolved. Critics of the volunteer force had been pointing to a perceived deterioration in the quality of volunteers during the period, as gauged by

---

and Inactive/Former Participants in the Post-Vietnam Era Veterans' Educational Assistance Program: Results and Conclusions, FR-ETSD-80-1 (Alexandria, Va.: Human Resources Research Organization, 1980). It is estimated that no more than 15 percent of service members who are eligible for VEAP will ever attend school as veterans receiving VEAP benefits. See Congressional Budget Office, *Improving Military Educational Benefits: Effects on Costs, Recruiting, and Retention*, prepared by Daniel Huck, Lorin Kusmin, and Edward Shepard (GPO, 1982), p. 15.

18. Hunter and Nelson, "Eight Years with the All-Volunteer Armed Forces," p. 97.

19. Ibid., p. 101.

20. Ibid., p. 99.

21. U.S. Department of Defense, Office of the Assistant Secretary of Defense, *Aptitude Testing of Recruits*, report to the House Committee on Armed Services (DOD, 1980), p. 10.

such measures as reading ability, on-the-job test scores, and attrition rates, at the same time that proponents were brandishing statistics showing that record-low proportions of below-average recruits were being attracted. The degree to which recruitment results would have been affected had the test scores been properly calibrated will never be known, but, according to a Pentagon report, "The efforts of recruiters might have resulted in the enlistment of more highly qualified individuals, and the average scores might not have declined so dramatically when renormed."[22]

In any event, alarmed by these developments, Congress enacted legislation in 1980 that limited to 25 percent the proportion of new recruits who score in the lowest AFQT category and to 35 percent the proportion of new Army recruits who have not completed high school.[23] At the same time, Congress enacted sizable increases in pay and benefits intended to shore up inadequate military wages and spur recruitment of higher-quality youth. Among them were an 11.7 percent across-the-board increase in military basic pay and allowances and a substantial increase in the number and size of enlistment bonuses; the overall increase in average military compensation was about 17 percent in that year. Combined with the 14.3 percent increase granted in 1981, the pay of members of the armed forces was raised by roughly one-third in just two years.[24]

This was accompanied by a deepening of the recession and further deterioration in the civilian employment prospects of American youth. The unemployment rate among sixteen- to nineteen-year-old males climbed to 19.6 percent by 1981. Furthermore, an improved educational benefits package was made available to Army enlistees who met certain qualifications, in effect raising the maximum amount of educational benefits to $20,100 (including $2,700 contributed by the participant).[25] The Army also intensified its recruiting efforts by expanding its advertising programs, adding recruiters, and shifting some from urban areas to suburban locations near high school and college campuses in an effort

22. U.S. Department of Defense, Office of the Assistant Secretary of Defense for Manpower, Reserve Affairs, and Logistics, *Profile of American Youth: 1980 Nationwide Administration of the Armed Services Vocational Aptitude Battery* (DOD, 1982), note 3 on p. 19.

23. Department of Defense Authorization Act, 1981, sec. 302, 94 Stat. 1082.

24. U.S. Department of Defense, *Manpower Requirements Report, FY 1984* (DOD, 1983), pp. ix–4.

25. CBO, *Improving Military Educational Benefits*, p. 17.

to obtain "better" recruits.[26] Finally, a reduction in the required number of new recruits—largely as a consequence of improved retention—helped the Army; compared to fiscal 1980 when about 157,000 volunteers had to be recruited, the Army enlisted only 117,000 and 118,000 in fiscal years 1981 and 1982, respectively.

The separate influences of these changes cannot be measured with precision, but together they worked, as the qualitative characteristics of recruits improved markedly beginning in 1981. As shown in table 2, the services recruited an unprecedented proportion of high school graduates and effected a sharp improvement in the aptitude profile. The turnaround was especially important for the Army, which had experienced the greatest difficulties in the late 1970s (see table 3).

Here again, the influence of expanded participation by women on overall personnel quality was evident, as indicated by the following comparison of test score distributions of Army recruits who entered between fiscal years 1974 and 1983:

AFQT category	Men	Women
I	2.3	5.2
II	21.4	37.3
III	47.0	43.4
IV	29.3	14.1

During the initial period (fiscal years 1974-76), women made up 9 percent of the Army's recruits but accounted for 30 percent of all volunteers in AFQT category I and less than 1 percent of those in category IV. Between fiscal years 1977 and 1980, although women recruits did not escape the test calibration problems discussed earlier, their qualitative advantage persisted, albeit somewhat narrowed; women made up 12 percent of Army volunteers, while constituting about 16 percent of category I recruits and just over 7 percent of category IV enlistees. As additional numbers of qualified men have entered the Army since the recruitment turnaround in the early 1980s, the impact of women has lessened. Between 1981 and 1983 women made up 13 percent of Army volunteers and 14 percent of category I recruits, but still only 7 percent of all enlistees in category IV.[27]

26. Larry Carney, "Recruiters Will Move Nearer to Campuses," *Army Times,* September 7, 1981.

27. Derived from data provided by the Defense Manpower Data Center.

Table 4. Military Enlisted Personnel Turnover Rates,[a] by Service, Selected Fiscal Years, 1955–83

Percent

Service	Draft era		Volunteer era		
	1955–65	*1966–73*	*1974–77*	*1978–80*	*1981–83*
Army	26	35	26	20	18
Navy	17	19	20	18	17
Marine Corps	19	33	29	23	22
Air Force	14	16	14	15	15
Total	20	26	22	18	17

Sources: Fiscal years 1955–80 end strengths from U.S. Department of Defense, *Selected Manpower Statistics, Fiscal Year 1980* (DOD, 1979); for fiscal years 1981–83 see *Budget of the United States Government, Fiscal Year 1983—Appendix; 1984; 1985.* Enlistment data for fiscal years 1955–59, *Selected Manpower Statistics, Fiscal Year 1970*, p. 42; fiscal years 1960–72, *Selected Manpower Statistics, Fiscal Year 1973*, p. 50; and fiscal years 1973–83, Defense Manpower Data Center.

a. Turnover rates are the number of new entrants (inductee or enlistee) in a given year as a percentage of the total end strength at the beginning of the year.

Retention of Skilled Personnel

One of the dividends expected to flow from abolishing the draft was a reduction in personnel turnover as volunteers would be serving longer initial enlistments than draftees and would be more likely to "go career." It was hoped that fewer new recruits would be needed each year, training and travel costs would be reduced, and the experience level of the force would be raised.

However, as table 4 reveals, the benefits were slow to be realized. For the first several years after the draft, overall personnel turnover (percentage replaced during the year) dropped below that experienced just before the end of the draft, but remained higher than the turnover during the more representative pre-Vietnam peacetime period. Although volunteers were signing up to serve for longer than the two years required of their conscripted predecessors, a relatively large proportion was washing out of training or otherwise failing to fulfill enlisted contracts. For example, of those males who enlisted for three or more years in fiscal 1974, 37 percent were discharged before completing three years, compared with 26 percent of the cohort that had enlisted in fiscal 1971.[28] The higher rate of losses was largely a consequence of policies designed to identify and separate as early as possible volunteers who could not

28. U.S. Department of Defense, Office of the Assistant Secretary of Defense for Manpower, Reserve Affairs, and Logistics, *America's Volunteers: A Report on the All-Volunteer Armed Forces* (DOD, 1978), p. 65. As the report points out, this increased the requirement for new recruits in fiscal 1974 by 17 percent.

adapt to military life. The trend was reversed once management attention was directed toward the issue; among the males who enlisted for three or more years in fiscal 1980, about 31 percent were discharged before completing three years.[29] Turnover was expected to drop further because cohorts after fiscal 1980 have had larger proportions of high school graduates, who have been more likely than dropouts to complete their obligated term of service.

At the same time that the early attrition situation appeared to be under control, concerns were being voiced about the loss of experienced troops, described as a "hemorrhage of talent" by the Chief of Naval Operations. Amidst reports of ships being tied up and aircraft being grounded for lack of skilled specialists and technicians, senior military officers were testifying before Congress that "the armed services are rapidly losing their best and most experienced personnel."[30] Particularly troublesome were falling rates of reenlistment among "careerists"— those who had already demonstrated, by reenlisting after an initial enlistment, an interest in pursuing a military career.[31] The proportion of careerists who chose to reenlist, which had been running at close to 83 percent when the draft ended, dropped to under 69 percent by fiscal 1979. Although the extent to which these figures signified a real problem remains controversial, they nevertheless contributed to the accumulating views that the nation's armed forces were in trouble.[32]

By the turn of the decade, however, reenlistment rates had recovered, increasing only modestly at first but reaching 77 percent by fiscal 1981. Although shortages of experienced personnel in certain occupational areas continued to be reported, by 1982 the military services were no

29. Data provided by Defense Manpower Data Center.

30. Richard Halloran, "Armed Forces Chiefs Say Personnel Losses Weaken U.S. Defense," *New York Times*, March 22, 1980.

31. Reenlistment rates are the proportions of "eligibles" who reenlist. Not everyone is eligible to reenlist; for example, effective January 1, 1982, the Army denied reenlistment to soldiers who failed to make grade E-4 (corporal or specialist four) during their first three years of service, first-term soldiers with certain disciplinary incidents on their record, or those who had failed to attain a minimum score on their entry test. See Larry Carney, "Re-up Bar Tightened for 18-Year Troops," *Army Times*, January 4, 1982.

32. Reenlistment rates are only one measure of changes in the experience level of the armed forces. Other measures include the actual *number* of reenlistments, retention rates (the number of reenlistments divided by the total number eligible to separate), continuation rates (the percentage of those in the military at the beginning of a year who were still in the ranks at the end of the year), and the "career/first term mix"— the ratio of the number of "career" personnel (those with four or more years of service) to the number of "first termers" (those with less than four years of service).

Table 5. Average Armed Forces Qualification Test Scores, by Enlisted Grade and Service, December 1982

	Service				
Grade	*Army*	*Navy*	*Air Force*	*Marine Corps*	*All services*
E-1	51	52	60	54	53
E-2	51	52	59	55	53
E-3	47	56	60	51	54
E-4	41	59	58	53	51
E-5	47	63	61	56	56
E-6	53	62	60	60	58
E-7	55	66	65	57	60
E-8	52	67	66	63	59
E-9	54	67	67	53	62

Source: Derived from data provided by Defense Manpower Data Center.

longer complaining about significant retention problems, and, as table 4 reveals, all of the services except the Air Force registered improvements in turnover rates during 1981-83. Apparently military pay increases and the deepening recession of the early 1980s not only accounted for gains in recruitment, but for many made the military a more attractive career alternative.[33]

Not only had retention problems lessened; in fact, the Army was trying to find ways to hold down reenlistments, at least among certain groups. As a legacy of its recruitment problems in the late 1970s, the Army's pool of potential reenlistees in the early 1980s was dominated by low-aptitude soldiers. In fiscal year 1982, for example, close to half the soldiers who had originally scored below the thirty-first percentile on the entry test and who were eligible reenlisted, and in early fiscal 1983 the low scorers constituted over 50 percent of all soldiers eligible to reenlist.[34] The net effects for the aptitude profile for all the services can be seen in table 5. The low aptitude scores of junior noncommissioned officers (grades E-4 and E-5), especially in the Army, is worrisome, since these individuals are today's trainers and tomorrow's supervisors. It should be noted, however, that the significance of *entry* test scores

33. The emphasis recently placed on providing larger percentage increases in pay to those in the upper ranks is more helpful for retention than for recruitment. The *average* raise in fiscal 1982, for example, was 14.3 percent, but the increases ranged from 10 percent for recruits to 17 percent for the top enlisted grades. Also, the 4 percent raise in January 1984 was given to everyone except recruits.

34. Larry Carney, "Unit Reenlistment Boards Weighted for 1st-Termers," *Army Times*, November 29, 1982.

diminishes—and measures of actual performance increase—as the soldier gains on-the-job experience. Whether or not these low-aptitude cohorts create problems as they advance to higher grades in an increasingly technological Army remains to be seen.

The Mobilization Problem

Concurrent with the abolition of peacetime conscription was an important modification in defense planning concepts: whereas U.S. conventional forces in the early 1960s had been based on a "two-and-a-half-war" scenario, the forces of the 1970s would be structured for one-and-a-half wars. The former concept assumed that two major nonnuclear contingencies (for example, in Europe and Korea) and one lesser contingency (for example, Cuba) could arise simultaneously. This was modified in 1970 by dropping a major planning contingency, a decision based largely on diminished prospects of a two-front attack by Russia and China. Conventional forces were to be structured "for simultaneously meeting a major Communist attack in either Europe or Asia, assisting allies against non-Chinese threats in Asia, and contending with a contingency elsewhere."[35] Thus the Nixon administration justified a reduced need for U.S. conventional forces and cut back active-duty Army divisions, tactical air wings, and fleet capabilities following the end of the U.S. military presence in Southeast Asia. The cause-and-effect relationships among the decisions to reduce planning contingencies, cut active force levels, and abolish conscription remain unclear.

A key element of the new security strategy was to be the concept of "total force planning," which placed a larger responsibility on the nation's military reserve forces. Much of the combat support for active units was moved to the reserves, and several reserve combat units—from battalion to brigade size—were affiliated with active Army divisions. In addition, active-duty units were to be manned at lower peacetime levels on the assumption that they would be filled out before deployment with members of the Individual Ready Reserve (IRR), who would be the principal source for initial combat replacements.[36]

---

35. Richard Nixon, *U.S. Foreign Policy for the 1970s: A New Strategy for Peace,* a report to the Congress (GPO, 1970), p. 129.

36. The Individual Ready Reserve is composed of those people who have served less than six years in active or reserve units (and thus have a residual obligation), are

The extent to which the "total force" concept was taken seriously during the early 1970s is open to debate. During the transition to the all-volunteer force, it became evident that reserve units, which had experienced little difficulty filling their ranks with draft-induced "volunteers," would have trouble adapting to the end of conscription. Strengths of the Army Reserve and National Guard sagged as the queue of applicants dissolved. Moreover, the Individual Ready Reserve, which had topped 1.2 million in 1973, was half that size by 1975.

Despite the rhetoric about the importance of the reserves, these shortages were discounted largely on the grounds that a conventional war would not last long enough for the reserves to matter anyway. The "short war" school of thought contended that a future conventional conflict would be measured in terms of days or weeks, rather than months or years, ending early in either negotiations or escalation to nuclear war. "Except under very optimistic assumptions about the time required for [Warsaw] Pact mobilization and deployment," wrote Secretary of Defense James R. Schlesinger in 1974, "the upshot is that the majority of Army Guard and Reserve units cannot play a role in the early and critical stages of a war in Central Europe."[37]

Toward the end of the 1970s, prompted by changing estimates of Soviet capabilities to sustain a longer war and by the lessons of the 1973 Arab-Israeli war, the demands of an intense protracted conventional conflict in Europe were reassessed. In 1978 a test of the nation's mobilization capabilities revealed that, should the forces of NATO and the Warsaw Pact square off in a replay of World War II, the Army would soon run short of combat troops. Accordingly, mobilization capabilities received more attention, and concerns about the reserve forces were taken more seriously. Through a set of new initiatives, including bonuses and educational incentives, by 1980 shortfalls in the Army National Guard and the Army Reserve had been noticeably reduced, and the Pentagon was optimistic that the gap could be completely closed by 1985.[38]

Shortages in the Army's IRR, on the other hand, remained substan-

not members of units, and generally do not train or get paid. They are liable to call-up and would be used to fill out active units upon mobilization and as combat replacements. U.S. Department of Defense, *America's Volunteers*, p. 223.

37. *Annual Defense Department Report, FY 1976*, p. 96.

38. Robert B. Pirie, "The All-Volunteer Force Today: Mobilization Manpower" in Goodpaster, Elliott, and Hovey, eds., *Toward a Consensus on Military Service*, p. 120.

tial—estimated at 270,000 in 1979.[39] Several measures were initiated in the early 1980s to expand the IRR: bonuses were offered, women were included for the first time, and provisions allowing for transfer from the IRR into the Standby Reserve (a less mobilizable reserve category) were tightened. The Department of Defense was hopeful that these steps would yield an Army IRR strength of 400,000 by 1985, which would reduce the shortfall to about 80,000; others remained skeptical.[40] At any rate, concerns about the Army's mobilization potential persisted into the early 1980s and marred otherwise optimistic assessments that the all-volunteer force could fulfill the nation's security needs.

Social Composition

One of the more persistent concerns about the all-volunteer force has been its failure to attract a representative cross section of the population. The case for representation in the armed forces has been argued from several perspectives. One school of thought has expressed concern that a military not broadly representative of society would foster its own rigid ethos and weaken civilian control; this group fears that a "professional" rather than a "citizen" army would become isolated from community values and less concerned about the ethics of its own use.[41] Another group of critics argues that representativeness is somehow related to military effectiveness; in a conscripted force, "middle-class and upwardly mobile youth helped enrich the skill level and commitment of military units in peace as well as in war."[42] The case has also been advanced on social equity grounds. Senator Ernest F. Hollings, Democrat of South Carolina, was outspoken on the issue before a group of students at Dartmouth College in November 1983:

39. A good deal of controversy surrounds IRR shortages, which have been placed anywhere between zero and 350,000. The principal disagreements stem from different assumptions concerning "no-show" rates (the percentage who, for one reason or another, would fail to report upon mobilization) and casualty rates. See ibid., pp. 126-27.

40. Ibid., p. 128.

41. See, for example, Morris Janowitz, "The U.S. Forces and the Zero Draft," *Adelphi Papers*, no. 94 (London: International Institute for Strategic Studies, 1973), pp. 27-29; and the President's Commission on an All-Volunteer Armed Force, *The Report of the President's Commission on an All-Volunteer Armed Force* (Macmillan, 1970), pp. 130-31.

42. Charles C. Moskos, "Social Considerations of the All-Volunteer Force," in Scowcroft, ed., *Military Service in the United States*, p. 136.

I want to draft everyone in this room for the good of the country. . . . Conscience tells us that we need a cross section of America in our armed forces. Defense is everybody's business. . . . A professional Army is un-American. It is anathema to a democratic republic—a glaring civil wrong.[43]

"We are relying excessively on the poor of this country," echoed Representative Paul Simon, Democrat of Illinois. "When blood is shed in Grenada or Lebanon or anywhere else, it is the poor of the country whose blood is shed. There are no sons of members of Congress or members of the Cabinet in Grenada or Lebanon."[44]

Whether these criticisms are valid is difficult to determine, since there is little agreement on a definition of "middle class"; moreover, the armed services do not routinely collect information on some of the generally accepted socioeconomic class indicators—income, occupation, and educational attainment of parents.

A comparison of family income of male recruits with the relevant civilian population on the basis of address zip codes indicated that volunteers who entered the armed forces during the first several years without the draft were "somewhat skewed toward the lower-income group relative to the distribution of all 16 to 21 year old males." The differences were most conspicuous in the higher-income range; for example, only 8 percent of the male volunteers came from the upper 10 percent of all zip codes (based on average family income), compared with close to 14 percent of all sixteen- to twenty-one-year-old males.[45]

But, as the study concluded, this was nothing new. A comparison of these volunteers with inductees and volunteers of the draft era verified the self-evident: the military has traditionally drawn a disproportionately small number of young men from upper-income groups. The study concluded that the fears that the all-volunteer force would become an "army of the poor" were groundless.[46]

These results were generally supported by a Pentagon survey in 1975, which confirmed that the family income situation of volunteers was not appreciably out of line with that of the population, except in the upper-income range.[47] This pattern is also evident when comparing other socioeconomic characteristics of male military personnel and their

---

43. Mark Shields, "The Candid Candidate," *Washington Post*, November 25, 1983.

44. *Congressional Record*, daily edition (November 16, 1983), p. H10029.

45. Richard V. L. Cooper, *Military Manpower and the All-Volunteer Force* (Santa Monica: Rand Corp., 1977), pp. 226-27.

46. Ibid., p. 230.

47. U.S. Department of Defense, *America's Volunteers*, p. 44.

Table 6. Selected Characteristics of Males in Full-Time Employment, the Armed Forces, and College, Ages Eighteen to Twenty-one, 1979
Percent unless otherwise indicated

Characteristic	Full-time employment[a]	Armed forces	College
Education of parent			
Less than twelve years	26	23	8
Twelve years	50	45	30
Thirteen years or more	24	32	62
Occupation of parent[b]			
Professional or managerial	22	23	56
Sales, clerical	12	11	13
Blue-collar	53	52	24
Service	8	12	6
Educational expectations			
Less than twelve years	11	2	. . .
Twelve years	49	27	. . .
Thirteen to fifteen years	25	26	8
Sixteen years or more	16	46	92
Knowledge of World of Work, mean score[c]	6.8	6.9	7.7

Source: Derived from Choongsoo Kim and others, "The All-Volunteer Force: An Analysis of Youth Participation, Attrition, and Reenlistment," prepared for the Employment and Training Administration, U.S. Department of Labor (Ohio State University, Center for Human Resource Research, 1980), pp. 17, 94, 98, 111. Figures are rounded.

a. Excludes those who still attend high school or are enrolled in college full time.

b. Excludes farming.

c. Knowledge of World of Work is a test in which respondents are asked to identify the kinds of work done in nine occupations. The scores indicate how many occupations were correctly identified.

civilian counterparts. As table 6 shows, in the late 1970s the family characteristics and educational expectations of armed forces personnel compared favorably with full-time civilian workers in the same age group, but both groups fell considerably short of the college-going population by any of the measures.

But sharp differences were found among the individual services: the Navy and Air Force were attracting young men with "better" backgrounds and "better" credentials than those in the civilian work force, while the reverse was true for the Army and Marine Corps.[48] This is not surprising, because the Navy and Air Force traditionally have been able to maintain stricter entrance standards that virtually ensure that by almost any measurement their recruits are of higher caliber. Recent improvements in the quality of Army and Marine Corps recruits may lead to a lessening of these differences.

48. Derived from data provided by Defense Manpower Data Center.

In a similar vein, some people are worried that future national leaders will be less likely than their predecessors to have served in the armed forces. "When so few of those making choices about military policy have first-hand exposure to the military," wrote James Fallows, "it increases the risk that they will be buffaloed, either by the services or by equally passionate groups on the left, and virtually eliminates the possibility that they will bring their own, uncoached sense of nuance and perspective to the military reports they hear."[49]

The merits of the situation aside, it is clear that, under the volunteer system, chances are slim that future leaders will have served in the nation's armed forces, especially in the enlisted ranks. Since the end of the draft, the connection between the military and higher education communities—considered by many to be one of the important links between the nation's armed forces and its society—has weakened. Indeed, one of the consequences of raising armed forces by strictly voluntary means has been a confirmation that the clienteles of the nation's military and higher education institutions are, for the most part, mutually exclusive groups. As self-evident as that might appear, the distinction was blurred during the postwar conscription era when many college men served not only as commissioned officers, as has been traditional, but also in the military's rank and file. During the same period, military veterans constituted a substantial part of college student bodies.

During the 1960s, for example, about 15 percent of the men entering the armed forces in an enlisted status had already acquired some college experience, and approximately 35 percent of the veterans leaving the service entered college-level programs under the GI bill. In the early 1980s, by contrast, only 7 percent of military volunteers had some college experience, and less than 5 percent of the veterans leaving the services were enrolling at the college level.[50] If current patterns continue, close

49. James Fallows, *National Defense* (Random House, 1981), p. 137.

50. Veteran enrollments in college-level institutions peaked at 1.9 million in fiscal year 1976, when veterans (largely of the Vietnam war) constituted 17.5 percent of total enrollments. Veteran enrollments dropped to about 840,000 by 1980, when veterans accounted for less than 7 percent of the college population. See U.S. Veterans Administration, Statistical Review and Analysis Division, *Historical Data on the Usage of Educational Benefits, 1944-1980*, IB 04-81-8 (VA, 1981). This trend can be expected to continue since the vast majority of Vietnam-era veterans likely to use their benefits have already done so, and by all indications the participation rate by veterans who have attained eligibility since enactment of the 1976 legislation will be relatively low. Pre-

Figure 1. Relationship between Educational Attainment and Military Service

Number per 1,000 males
and percent of preceding group

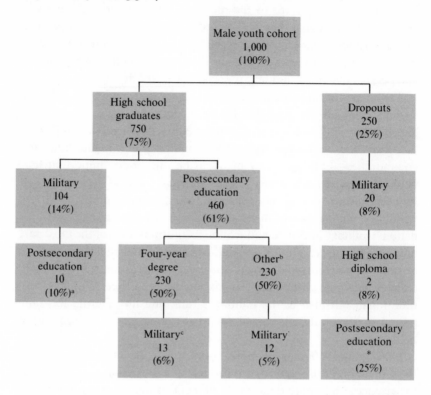

Sources: Rates of educational attainment from W. Vance Grant and Leo J. Eiden, *Digest of Educational Statistics, 1982,* U.S. Department of Education, National Center for Educational Statistics (Government Printing Office, 1982), p. 15. Military participation rates derived from data provided by Defense Manpower Data Center, 1984. Estimates of military veterans entering postsecondary education obtained from Veterans Administration, 1984. Estimates of the percentage of dropouts who enter the armed forces, subsequently acquire a high school diploma, and enter a postsecondary program from Richard V. L. Cooper, "Military Manpower Procurement Policy and the Supply of Scientists and Engineers," in National Research Council, *The Effect of Military Personnel Requirements on the Future Supply of Scientists and Engineers in the United States* (National Academy Press, 1981), p. 25.
  * Fewer than one.
  a. Although recent data indicate that fewer than 5 percent of military veterans are enrolling in college-level programs, the participation rate is expected to increase for future veterans who will be eligible for more liberal educational benefits, such as the Army College Fund.
  b. Graduates of two-year programs and dropouts.
  c. College graduates who enter the armed forces generally do so as commissioned officers.

to half of all American men will attend a college-level program and roughly 15 percent will serve in the military, but less than 4 percent will do both (see figure 1). On the other hand, if a broad-based noncontributory GI bill is restored (a possibility discussed below), and the benefits are utilized at the Vietnam-era rate, the proportion of the male population who over the long run would both serve in the military and attend college could be expected to exceed 8 percent.

One of the most conspicuous changes in the social composition of the armed forces has been in the racial mix.[51] Whereas just before the end of the draft black membership in the enlisted ranks of the nation's ground forces was roughly in line with the eligible population (about 12 percent), by 1981 the proportion had reached just over 33 percent in the Army and 22 percent in the Marine Corps. Growth in the black membership of the Air Force and Navy enlisted ranks was far more modest: by 1981 black representation in the Navy was about equal to the black proportion of the military-age population and in the Air Force it was slightly over that. At the same time, the proportion of black officers in the armed forces remained noticeably out of balance despite a more than twofold increase over the period, from 2.3 percent in 1972 to just over 5 percent in 1981.

This situation, the result of a variety of social and economic factors not necessarily related to voluntary recruitment, has given rise to a number of worries—some held predominantly by whites, others held predominantly by blacks, and some shared by members of both groups. Much of the uneasiness may simply be reaction to a change from racial "proportionality"—a situation that is generally understandable and acceptable to all population subgroups. But there are specific concerns as well.

Fielding combat forces composed of an overproportion of blacks, some say, imposes an unfair burden on one segment of American society, a burden that seems particularly inequitable because members of that group have not enjoyed a fair share of the benefits that the state confers. Thus by this argument the prospect that at least one-third of the combat fatalities in the early phases of a military engagement would be suffered

---

liminary data obtained from the Veterans Administration indicate, for example, that of roughly 715,000 service members who had separated from the military by the end of fiscal 1983 and who were eligible for VEAP educational assistance, only 33,170 had enrolled in a college-level program.

51. Discussion and data for the next three paragraphs are from Binkin and Eitelberg, *Blacks and the Military,* especially pp. 42, 66, and table A-1.

by black soldiers or marines is immoral, unethical, or somehow contrary to the precepts of democratic institutions.

But not everyone agrees. Many Americans look with approval on the growth of black participation in military service, since it affords young blacks educational, social, and financial opportunities that constitute a bridge to a better life not otherwise available to them. The fact that two of every five eligible young black males have been entering the volunteer military indicates its importance to them as an employer.

The trend toward greater racial imbalance appeared to turn around in the early 1980s. After reaching an all-time high of close to 37 percent in 1979, the proportion of black Army recruits started to drop in 1980 and was down to 22 percent by 1983—still exceeding the proportion of the eligible black population, but clearly a reversal of the trend of 1973-79. In absolute terms, fewer blacks entered the Army in fiscal 1983 than in any one-year period since the end of conscription, and fewer black males did so than since the early 1960s.

The sudden reversal in the black enlistment rate is the obvious consequence of an increased interest in the military on the part of white youths resulting from worsening conditions in the job market, large increases in entry-level military pay, and enlistment incentives that favor whites (such as supplementary educational benefits targeted to volunteers with above-average aptitude scores).[52]

Unit Cohesion

Finally, it has been argued that the very programs that the Pentagon has implemented to make the volunteer system work have weakened the cohesiveness that is essential to an effective fighting force. The emphasis on "occupational" policies that accompanied the end of conscription, according to a leading critic, has redefined military service in terms of the economic marketplace. One of the principal casualties has been the traditional military lifestyle, the centerpiece of which was "barracks life." In an earlier era, when cash pay was extremely low,

---

52. This is not meant to imply that racial discrimination exists. But, under current entry standards, a great deal depends on aptitude test scores. As matters stand, if cutoff scores are set at a point at which 50 percent of whites qualify, then only about 16 percent of black Americans will qualify. For a more extended discussion, see ibid., especially pp. 87-98.

most junior people were single and ate at the mess hall and lived with their unit on post. Today, however, many volunteers, with higher levels of disposable income, are often married and choose to eat and to live on the civilian economy. This change, so the argument goes, has undermined unit camaraderie and has diminished military effectiveness.[53]

The expanded participation of women in the armed forces, hastened by the end of conscription, has also been viewed as a flaw in the volunteer concept. "The large-scale introduction of women in the armed forces," wrote one critic, "subverts discipline and morale." Military cohesiveness, he contended, "is best fostered in all-male groups, for in mixed groups various extraneous and destructive impulses begin to work— sexual desire or envy, pity, and misogyny among them."[54] "The disadvantages of using women," according to another conscription advocate, "far outweigh the advantages. Training regimens . . . have been watered down. Sexual attractions dissipate a unit's sense of mission. . . . Double standards in performance and discipline have unavoidably evolved."[55] And the issue of pregnancy has been continuously raised. By one account, "It became common to see obviously pregnant soldiers at missile batteries in West Germany or pregnant sailors aboard Navy supply ships. Seven to 10 percent of all service women, married or unmarried, became pregnant in the course of a year."[56]

Emotional pleas aside, little is known in fact about the effects that women are having on cohesiveness, in part because cohesiveness is an intangible that lacks an agreed-upon measurement. To the extent that disciplinary statistics, namely absenteeism and desertion, are indicative of group cohesiveness, the introduction of women into the ranks has not had adverse effects. In 1980, for example, rates of absenteeism and desertion among Army personnel were 70 to 75 percent below those

53. Charles C. Moskos, "How to Save the All-Volunteer Force," *The Public Interest*, no. 61 (Fall 1980), p. 83. Moskos points out that close to half of all enlisted men in the Army in 1983 were married, compared with one-fourth when the draft ended in 1973. Charles C. Moskos, "The Enlisted Man in the All-Volunteer Army" (Northwestern University, Department of Sociology, January 1984), p. 6.

54. Eliot A. Cohen, "Why We Need a Draft," *Commentary*, vol. 73 (April 1982), pp. 38-39.

55. James Webb, "The Draft: Why the Army Needs It," *The Atlantic Monthly* (April 1980), p. 38.

56. Charles C. Moskos, Jr., and Peter Braestrup, "The Human Element," *The Wilson Quarterly* (Winter 1983), p. 135.

experienced in 1972, the year that the expansion in the role of women was launched.[57]

Summary: The First Decade

The first ten years following the end of conscription have been turbulent ones for the nation's military establishment. Throughout the period, the armed forces remained very near their authorized strengths, which were modestly but continuously declining. But at times the quantity of manpower was obtained at the expense of quality; this was particularly evident in the Army in the late 1970s as it unknowingly accepted large numbers of volunteers who, it would later learn, did not meet prescribed entry standards. At the same time, all of the military services were expressing concern about heavy losses of experienced specialists, technicians, and supervisors. Moreover, there seemed to be little progress in dealing with the manning shortages that had plagued the Army reserve forces since the end of conscription. And finally, the racial composition of the nation's ground forces was becoming increasingly unrepresentative of the American population. By the end of the seventies, the nation appeared close to considering a return to conscription.

But new military pay raises, intensified recruiting efforts, a depressed civilian job market, and, by some accounts, a surge in national pride have combined to make the early 1980s something of a success for the all-volunteer force. The services recruited record proportions of high school graduates, and retention problems seemed to all but disappear. However, concerns about organizational cohesion, racial balance, and manpower mobilization capabilities persist and still serve as the broadsword of those who would prefer to see a revival of the draft. But these concerns, in themselves, have not been considered serious enough to put the volunteer concept in jeopardy. Moreover, in the absence of convincing evidence that proposed alternatives to the current volunteer system would improve the effectiveness of the nation's armed forces, the burden of proof, which obviously lies with the critics of the status quo, has not been met.

57. Data provided by Office of Assistant Secretary of Defense for Manpower, Reserve Affairs, and Logistics.

Prospects for the Second Decade

As difficult as the first ten years may have been for the all-volunteer concept, the second decade could prove even more challenging as the armed forces face the possibility of being squeezed between a declining supply of qualified volunteers and an increasing demand for them.

Changes in the Youth Population

The manning problems experienced in the 1970s would have been less distressing had conditions been unfavorable for military recruitment. But a bumper crop of prospects—products of the baby boom—reached military age during the decade; in fact, there were more eighteen-year-olds in 1979 than at any other time in American history. Ironically, this was the same period in which the armed forces ran into their most difficult recruitment problems. The demographic depression of the 1980s and 1990s, then, is a cause for concern.

SMALLER NUMBERS. Dwindling birthrates in the United States—a trend that started in the late 1950s and brought the baby boom to an end in the mid-1960s—are having a significant impact on many areas of public policy.[58] As the "birth-dearth" generation passes through its formative years, the effects are already being felt, most notably by the nation's primary and secondary educational institutions. As the first cohorts of that generation completed high school, starting in about 1983, higher education institutions and the civilian labor force began to notice the effects, as did the armed forces, which have traditionally attracted eighteen- to twenty-one-year-old volunteers. The magnitude of the change can be seen in table 7; compared with 1981 levels, there will be about 2.5 million fewer in this age group by 1987 and roughly 4 million fewer by 1995.[59]

58. Although both fertility rates (live births per 1,000 women fifteen to forty-four) and the number of births began a gradual decline in 1958, demographers seem to agree that the end of the baby boom did not occur until 1965, when the decline in both measures became more conspicuous.

59. Cohort size will begin to increase again after 1995, because the annual number of births began to rise in 1976. This is a result of a delayed "echo effect": there are more women, born during the baby boom, who are now of childbearing age. Once this generation passes that age, starting in the 1990s, annual births will decline once again, barring larger-than-expected increases in fertility rates.

**Table 7. Projected U.S. Population Aged Eighteen to Twenty-one, by Sex and Race,
Selected Years, 1981–95**

Thousands

Category	1981	1983	1985	1987	1989	1991	1993	1995
Male	8,617	8,356	7,820	7,356	7,404	7,196	6,703	6,608
White	7,281	7,010	6,509	6,085	6,098	5,863	5,405	5,329
Black	1,147	1,146	1,102	1,052	1,070	1,072	1,023	993
Other	189	199	210	219	236	261	275	285
Female	8,401	8,143	7,621	7,165	7,197	6,983	6,495	6,387
White	7,059	6,799	6,312	5,896	5,897	5,666	5,219	5,136
Black	1,168	1,160	1,116	1,067	1,080	1,076	1,022	990
Other	175	184	193	202	219	241	254	260
Total	17,018	16,499	15,441	14,521	14,601	14,179	13,198	12,995

Source: U.S. Bureau of the Census, *Current Population Reports*, series P-25, no. 704, "Projections of the Population of the United States: 1977 to 2050" (Government Printing Office, 1977), pp. 40–60. Figures are rounded.

CHANGES IN SOCIAL COMPOSITION. The sex composition of the smaller population of young Americans will change little through the projected period: men will continue to hold a slight edge, growing from 50.6 percent in 1981 to 50.9 percent in 1995. More noticeable is the shift that will occur in the racial and ethnic composition as minorities make up an increasing proportion of the population. Minorities will constitute 19.4 percent of all eighteen- to twenty-one-year-olds in 1995, compared with 15.7 percent in 1981. Nonblack minorities will register the largest relative growth over the period—from 2.2 percent to 4.3 percent.[60] Inasmuch as minorities have been less likely to complete high school, a decline in overall high school graduation rates in the coming years seems probable.

DECLINING ABILITIES. At the same time, the downward trend in the abilities of the younger generation of Americans, especially their intellectual capacity and basic academic skills, could also have implications for the military. The most widely cited evidence has been the dropoff in Scholastic Aptitude Test (SAT) scores since 1963. In that year the average score on the verbal section of the SAT was 478 and on the mathematics portion 502; by 1980 the verbal mean score had dipped to 424 and the math score to 466—the lowest in the history of the test.[61]

60. Bureau of the Census, *Current Population Reports*, series P-25, no. 704, "Projections of the Population of the United States: 1977 to 2050" (GPO, 1977), pp. 33, 41.

61. College Entrance Examination Board, *On Further Examination: Report of the Advisory Panel on the Scholastic Aptitude Test Score Decline* (New York: College Board, 1977), p. 6; and College Board, *National Report on College-Bound Seniors, 1983*.

This downward trend has not been confined to SAT scores. In fact, with the exceptions of the Law School Admission Test and the Natural Science Subtest of the American College Test (ACT), all major measurements of aptitude have exhibited a similar performance pattern, as shown in figure 2. Not surprisingly, military aptitude test results show similar tendencies. In the early 1970s about 48 percent of all applicants to the armed forces scored above the fiftieth percentile on the standardized aptitude test, but only 37 percent of the applicants who took the test in the late 1970s were in that category.[62]

The causes for the decline remain subjects of debate, with speculation centering on the changing population of test takers in terms of sex, race or ethnic category, age, and socioeconomic status. A variety of other factors have also been blamed, from changes in family configuration and the adoption of a permissive philosophy of education to more bizarre hypotheses, such as the effects of radioactive fallout, drug intake, and food additives.[63]

However, the rate of decline appears to have slowed since the late 1970s. A leveling off in SAT scores in 1981 followed by a slight improvement in 1982 is a particularly hopeful sign.[64] But whether this marks the start of an upward trend remains to be seen.

IMPLICATIONS FOR RECRUITMENT. The shrinking youth population, in itself, is bound to have important implications for recruitment. The dimensions of the problem can be seen in table 8, which shows the proportion of the "qualified and available" *male* youth population that would have to enlist if the active and reserve forces are to meet annual recruit requirements.[65] During 1984-88, for example, an average of

62. Brian K. Waters and Janice H. Lawrence, "A Comparison of Test Score Trends: Civilian versus Military Examinees and Recruits (1972-1981)," paper prepared for the 1982 annual convention of the American Psychological Association.

63. Brian K. Waters, "The Test Score Decline: A Review and Annotated Bibliography," Technical Memorandum 81-2, prepared for the Office of the Assistant Secretary of Defense for Manpower, Reserve Affairs, and Logistics (Alexandria, Va.: Human Resources Research Organization, 1981).

64. College Board, *National Report, 1983*.

65. The "qualified and available" pool excludes those who *cannot* volunteer and those who are *unlikely* to volunteer for military service. The former are individuals who would not be expected to meet minimum mental, physical, or moral standards. The latter includes college students who complete at least two years of college and individuals confined to various training, curative, or correctional institutions. The calculation here is confined to male youths since, under present policies, they will continue to constitute about 90 percent of all military personnel. Obviously, if the armed forces expanded the role of women beyond the current goals, a smaller proportion of the male population would have to be attracted. This possibility is discussed later.

Figure 2. Trends in Aptitude Measurements

Mean percentage change per year[a]

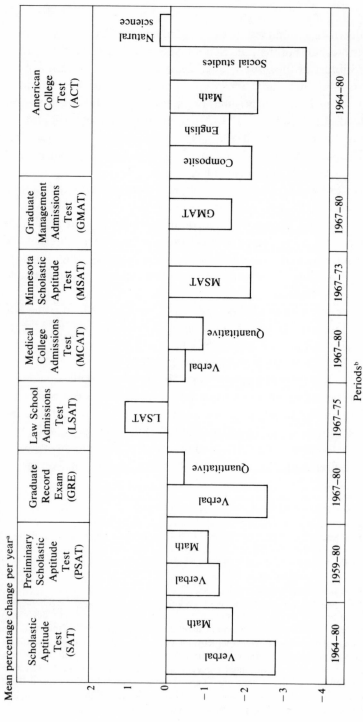

Periods[b]

Source: Brian K. Waters, "The Test Score Decline: A Review and Annotated Bibliography," Technical Memorandum 81-2, prepared for the Office of the Assistant Secretary of Defense for Manpower, Reserve Affairs, and Logistics (Alexandria, Va.: Human Resources Research Organization, 1981), p. 7.
a. Change expressed in terms of percentage of a standard deviation.
b. Time periods differ according to availability of data.

Table 8. Proportion of Qualified and Available Males Required for Military Service, Selected Periods, 1981–95
Thousands unless otherwise indicated

	Annual average		
Category	1981–83	1984–88	1991–95
Total eighteen-year-old males	**2,049**	**1,827**	**1,637**
Minus: Nonavailable	626	552	489
Institutionalized[a]	31	27	25
College enrollees less first- or second-year dropouts[b]	595	525	464
Minus: Unqualified	576	526	461
Mental[c]	363	337	291
Physical or moral[d]	213	189	170
Equals: Qualified and available male pool	**847**	**749**	**687**
Total male recruit requirements[e]	**354**	**376**	**376**
Active forces	270	278	278
Reserve forces	84	98	98
Percent of pool required	**42**	**50**	**55**

Sources: Total eighteen-year-old male population from U.S. Bureau of the Census, *Current Population Reports,* series P-25, no. 704, "Projections of the Population of the United States: 1977 to 2050." Institutionalized population estimates based on preliminary data from the 1980 census provided by Bureau of the Census, p. 15. College enrollment rates from W. Vance Grant and Leo J. Eiden, *Digest of Educational Statistics, 1982,* U.S. Department of Education, National Center for Educational Statistics (GPO, 1982), p. 15. First- and second-year dropouts based on estimates provided by National Center for Educational Statistics. Estimates of mentally and physically or morally unqualified derived from data contained in special tabulations provided by the Office of the Assistant Secretary of Defense for Manpower, Reserve Affairs, and Logistics. Male recruit requirements for fiscal years 1981–83 for active forces derived from data provided by Defense Manpower Data Center and for reserve forces from U.S. Department of Defense, *Official Guard and Reserve Manpower Strengths and Statistics, FY1981—Summary,* p. 167; *FY 1982—Summary,* p. 177; and *FY83—Summary,* p. 187. Male recruit requirements for fiscal years 1984 and beyond compiled from U.S. Department of Defense, Office of the Assistant Secretary of Defense for Manpower, Reserve Affairs, and Logistics, *Manpower Requirements Report, FY 1984* (DOD, 1983), pp. III-12, 20, 21; IV-10; V-7; VI-6, 9, 10. Projections of Navy and Marine Corps reserve requirements based on fiscal 1983 recruitment data.
  a. Assumes 1.5 percent of the male population aged eighteen to twenty-four is institutionalized.
  b. Estimates based on 1980 participation rates: in 1980, 74.4 percent of the youth cohort that had entered the fifth grade in 1972 completed high school and 46.3 percent of the initial group enrolled as full- or part-time students in programs creditable toward a bachelor's degree. Assumes that 25 percent of first-time enrollees leave during the first year and 12.5 percent during the second year.
  c. Based on 1981 military aptitude requirements, 2 percent of males with one or more years of college would be expected to be unqualified, 10 percent of high school graduates without college experience would not meet minimum standards, and 60 percent of non-high school graduates would not qualify.
  d. Assumes that 16.3 percent of the male youth population meeting minimum aptitude requirements would be disqualified on physical grounds and 3.9 percent would fail to meet moral standards.
  e. Assumes annual recruit requirements beyond fiscal 1984 will remain constant.

1,827,000 young men will be turning eighteen each year. Of these 525,000 are expected to enter college and complete at least two years, and, if the past is a guide, they would have a very low propensity for enlisted duty. Moreover, roughly the same number would not be expected to meet current mental, physical, or moral standards. During this period, then, the pool of qualified and available men will be filling by roughly 750,000 a year, out of which the armed forces will need to attract 376,000, or about half of them, to meet planned recruit requirements.[66] The situation will worsen in the early 1990s. As the table shows, about 60,000 fewer young men will be entering the qualified and available pool, and the armed forces will have to draw 55 percent, compared with 42 percent during 1981-83.

The task could well be understated, because the calculation is based on the assumptions that both the size of the armed forces and military entrance standards will remain the same and that a constant proportion of high school graduates will pursue higher education. Should the Reagan administration's blueprint for bolstering U.S. conventional power or anticipated advances in military technology come to pass, the armed services might have to enlist an even greater share of the relevant population. Moreover, should institutions of higher education attempt to increase their share of the smaller youth market to offset declining enrollments, the military's problems could be compounded.

The Prospective Military Buildup

While the Reagan administration remained "determined to meet . . . peacetime military manpower requirements with volunteers,"[67] its proposed defense program could involve a sizable growth in military manpower. The acquisition of a "600-ship Navy," for example, could swell by close to 50,000 the number of jobs for uniformed naval personnel. Planned improvements in the combat capabilities of Army forces could lead to an increase of as much as 35,000 in Army strength, and plans to add to the number of Air Force tactical fighter wings and to deploy cruise missiles in Europe could expand their manpower requirements by roughly 90,000.[68]

The expansion plans were stalled by budgetary pressures as the administration pared its fiscal year 1983 military manpower request by 10,000 before submitting it to Congress, which cut another 18,000.[69] The

66. To meet the recruit needs for the active forces alone, an average of 278,000 young men, or 37 percent of the qualified and available pool, will have to enlist each year.

67. *Department of Defense Annual Report to the Congress, Fiscal Year 1983*, p. III-161.

68. U.S. Department of Defense, Office of the Assistant Secretary of Defense for Manpower, Reserve Affairs, and Logistics, *Manpower Requirements Report, FY 1984*, (DOD, 1983), pp. III-4, IV-6, VI-1.

69. Charles W. Corddry, "Expansion of Military Hits Snags," *Baltimore Sun*, August 19, 1982.

Pentagon fared no better for fiscal 1984 as the Congress, apparently to encourage a larger role for the reserves, authorized only 10,500 of the 37,300 additional billets requested.[70] While the rate of buildup has been slowed, the administration apparently intends to pursue its manpower expansion plans, at least for the Air Force and Navy. In guidance provided by the Secretary of Defense for preparation of their fiscal year 1985-89 programs, the military services were instructed to plan to reach a military strength of about 2,270,000 by 1989, about 157,000 more than in 1983.[71] The Army, for its part, appears to have scrapped plans to increase its rolls, at least for fiscal 1985, choosing instead to create two new, smaller divisions within its authorized strength of about 780,000.[72]

Whether the increases envisioned by the administration can be accommodated under the volunteer system is problematical. In light of the recruiting successes of the early 1980s, some military officials were optimistic about attracting a substantial number of additional volunteers; the Army's chief of personnel, for example, expressed confidence that his service could expand its rolls to 850,000 without resorting to peace-time conscription.[73] The initial increases would probably be attainable under currently favorable recruitment conditions, but the resulting larger annual recruit flow would be more difficult to sustain over the long term. Other things remaining equal, adding 157,000 to the military rolls could be expected to increase the average annual requirement for male recruits by approximately 20,000, raising the total to 390,000, or close to 60 percent of the qualified and available population in the early 1990s.

Technology and Qualitative Standards

In addition to the prospect that the military services may have to attract *more* recruits is the possibility that they may have to seek *better* recruits: that is, those possessing aptitudes for absorbing more complex technical training. As the armed forces field increasingly sophisticated weapons systems, their requirements for specialists and technicians are expected to grow.

70. Tom Philpott, "Korb Says Personnel Curb Will Hurt Readiness," *Army Times,* August 29, 1983.

71. Richard Halloran, "Planning Memos Stress U.S. Show of Armed Force," *New York Times,* September 20, 1983.

72. Larry Carney, "Army Seeks 2 New, 2 Converted Light Divisions," *Army Times,* January 9, 1984.

73. Richard Halloran, "Army Personnel Chief Disputes Reports on Draft and Black Soldiers," *New York Times,* July 4, 1982.

Table 9. Distribution of Trained Military Enlisted Personnel, by Major Occupational Category, Selected Years, 1945–81
Percent

Major occupational category[a]	1945	1957	1981
White collar	28	40	47
Technical workers[b]	13	21	29
Clerical workers[c]	15	19	18
Blue collar	72[d]	60	55
Craftsmen[e]	29	32	28
Service and supply workers	17	13	11
Infantry, gun crews, and			
seamanship specialists	24	15	16

Sources: Data for 1945 and 1957, Harold Wool, *The Military Specialist: Skilled Manpower for the Armed Forces* (Johns Hopkins University Press, 1968), table III-3, p. 42. Data for 1981, provided by Office of the Assistant Secretary of Defense for Manpower, Reserve Affairs, and Logistics. Figures are rounded.
  a. Categories are based on the Department of Defense occupational classification system.
  b. Percentages for 1945 and 1957 include "electronics" and "other technical" categories. Percentage for 1981 includes "electronic equipment repairmen," "communications and intelligence specialists," "medical and dental specialists," and "other technical and allied specialists" categories.
  c. Percentages for 1945 and 1957 include administrative and clerical personnel. Percentage for 1981 is for the "functional support and administration" category.
  d. Includes 2 percent classified as miscellaneous.
  e. Percentages for 1945 and 1957 include "mechanics and repairmen" and "craftsmen" categories. Percentage for 1981 includes "electrical/mechanical equipment repairmen" and "craftsmen" categories.

The influence of technology on the military's skill mix in the postwar period is traced in table 9, which shows the conspicuous shift from work requiring general military skills toward tasks requiring special expertise. The sharpest changes have taken place in the jobs requiring technical skills (such as computer specialists, electronics technicians, or medical technicians), the service and supply occupations, and the general combat skills. The proportion of technical jobs, which has always been higher in the equipment-intensive Navy and Air Force, has markedly increased in the Army and, to a lesser extent, in the Marine Corps. For the Army, the increase in technical specialization has been at the expense of service and supply occupations and of combat skills.

These trends are likely to continue as new generations of weapons systems enter the inventory. With a growing emphasis on computerized command, control communications, and intelligence functions, new systems tend to be more complicated than their predecessors and serve to increase the number of skilled technicians and specialists in the military services.[74] A study of the impact of technology on naval aircraft

74. Theoretically, the introduction of new technologies need not increase either quantitative or qualitative manpower requirements. An argument could be made, for

systems concluded that "although new technology has improved component reliability (failures per part per flight hour), it has also permitted an increase in density of functions and capabilities (numbers of parts per system). This has resulted in overall decreases in system reliability and increases in maintenance manpower requirements."[75] The additional sailors needed to man the expanded fleet will have to meet stricter standards as the Navy's occupational mix adapts to high technology. By 1986, for example, "semi-technical" positions are expected to increase by 13 percent over 1981, "technical" billets by 16 percent, and "highly technical" jobs by 31 percent.[76] It is also estimated that the Air Force's need for people with high aptitudes for electronics skills will increase by about one-third by the year 2000.[77]

The impact that emerging technology will have on the Army's occupational mix and personnel standards is more difficult to identify. Unofficially, concerns have been expressed that, given the present course, the technologies that will be embodied in the Army's weapon systems of tomorrow may well be beyond the abilities of its manpower.[78] Some feel, in fact, that the potential performance of current weapon systems is degraded by the quality of today's soldiers. In a pessimistic

example, that technological advances could be applied to facilitate operations and maintenance rather than to extend capabilities. However, this has been the exception rather than the rule as "most often technical advance is used to stretch the performance of defense systems to the limit." See Seymour J. Deitchman, *New Technology and Military Power: General Purpose Military Forces for the 1980s and Beyond* (Westview Press, 1979), p. 266.

75. U.S. Department of the Navy, Personnel Research and Development Center, *Technology Trends and Maintenance Workload Requirements for the A-7, F-4, and F-14 Aircraft*, TR 79-19 (NPRDC, 1979), p. viii.

76. David Roehm, "The Developing Market for Military Manpower: Challenge," in Center for Naval Analyses, *Conference Proceedings of Naval Manpower Research in the 1980s* (Alexandria, Va.: CNA, 1982), p. 15. According to this analysis, the semitechnical jobs require an equal mix of AFQT category IIIA and IIIB groups, technical jobs call for two-thirds category III and one-third Category II people, and highly technical positions require, on average, those who score in category II.

77. Tidal W. McCoy, "U.S. Armed Forces Ill-Prepared for Today's Super-Sophisticated Weaponry," *Human Events* (October 21, 1982), pp. 10–11.

78. U.S. Army Support Center, *Soldier Capability–Army Combat Effectiveness* (SCACE), vol. 1: *Main Report*, prepared by Juri Toomepuu (Fort Benjamin Harrison, Ind.: USASSC, 1981); U.S Army Recruiting Command, "The Gideon Criterion: The Effects of Selection Criteria on Soldier Capabilities and Battle Results," Research Memorandum 82-1, prepared by J. Richard Wallace (Fort Sheridan, Ill.: USAREC, 1982); Thomas A. Horner, "Killers, Fillers, and Fodder," *Parameters*, vol. 12 (September 1982), pp. 27–34; and Dave Griffiths, "Incompetent GIs Man Army's Missile Posts," *Defense Week* (March 29, 1982).

assessment, General William Depuy (U.S. Army, retired) concluded that "the Army needs more quality than it has on board, more than it is now recruiting, [and] more than it can get under current policy or current budgets."[79] The issue has been under study within the Army, but results are unlikely to be available for several years. It has been suggested that, pending those findings, the Army adopt manpower standards that would provide an enlisted corps with a qualitative profile similar to that being recruited by the Air Force in the early 1980s.[80]

As the roster of technical jobs grows, the pool of qualified youth can be expected to shrink. In addition to the single index of general aptitude (AFQT), the entry test battery includes a variety of subtests that are combined to form composites designed to predict training success for clusters of occupations. The services use aptitude subtest results in different combinations tailored to their respective needs. To illustrate, the occupational areas for which composites are calculated by the Army and the subtests included in each are shown in table 10. To enter training as an infantryman, for example, an enlistee in 1981 needed a minimum score of 85 on the combat composite, while to qualify for training as an electronics instrument calibration specialist, a score of at least 120 on the electronics composite was required.[81] Based on these standards, about 72 percent of the American male youth population could be expected to qualify for infantry training while an estimated 25 percent would be eligible to enter calibration specialist training in the Army.[82] To the extent, then, that emerging military technology leads to a richer mix of technical skills, qualification rates can be expected to decline and

79. William E. Depuy, "The All-Volunteer Force (AVF)—The Demand Side—Army Perspective," paper prepared for a conference on "The AVF after a Decade: Retrospect and Prospect," U.S. Naval Academy, November 1983, p. 25.

80. U.S. Army Support Center, *Soldier Capability,* pp. 50-51.

81. Whether the standards used for enlistment, job classification, and assignment are as valid as the adherence to them implies is an open question. While it is generally acknowledged that aptitude test scores are valid predictors of training performance (as measured by paper-and-pencil tests),there is less agreement that they are related to job performance. Besides, some contend that advances in technology should not necessarily mean greater complexity. In fact, technology can make things simpler: "The new M1 Abrams tank is a far simpler machine for the gunner, the driver and the tank commander than the M4 Sherman tank of World War II; and the ability of today's gunner to get a first-round hit is far greater than it ever was for a Sherman gunner." [Comments of Gen. Frederick J. Kroesen, Commander in Chief, U.S. Army, Europe, *U.S. News and World Report* (August 9, 1982), p. 23.] For at least some jobs, psychomotor skills, demonstrated by the current generation's deftness with video games, may be at least as important as the cognitive skills measured by the current standardized entry tests.

82. Derived from data provided by Defense Manpower Data Center.

Table 10. Aptitude Subtest Components, by Army Occupational Area

Occupational area	Subtest components
Maintenance	General science, auto and shop information, mathematics knowledge, electronics information
Electronics	General science, arithmetic reasoning, mathematics knowledge, electronics information
Clerical	Numerical operations, coding speed, word knowledge
Mechanical maintenance	Numerical operations, auto and shop information, mechanical comprehension, electronics information
Surveillance and communications	Numerical operations, coding speed, auto and shop information, mechanical comprehension
Combat	Arithmetic reasoning, coding speed, auto and shop information, mechanical comprehension
Field artillery	Arithmetic reasoning, coding speed, mathematics knowledge, mechanical comprehension
Operator and food service	Numerical operations, auto and shop information, mechanical comprehension, word knowledge
Skilled technical	General science, mathematics knowledge, mechanical comprehension, word knowledge

Source: U.S. Department of Defense, "Manual for Administration: Armed Services Vocational Aptitude Battery, Forms 8, 9 and 10," DOD 1304.12M, October 1979.

recruitment to become more difficult. The adoption of the Air Force's minimum entrance standards by all of the military services, for example, would disqualify an additional 14 percent of the youth population and would increase from 53 percent to 68 percent the proportion of qualified and available male youths who would have to be attracted to meet projected military requirements in the early 1990s.

Competition from Higher Education

The relative scarcity of young people over the next decade will affect not only the military in ways described above, but all youth-dependent institutions, including higher education. Signs of nervousness are especially evident among educators as the nation's colleges and universities gear up for the upcoming competition.[83]

83. See, for example, Fred E. Crossland, "Learning to Cope with the Downward Slope," *Change* (July–August, 1980), pp.18-25; Cathy Henderson, "Competing for the Nation's Youth," *Educational Record* (Winter 1981), pp.59-67; and David W. Breneman, *The Coming Enrollment Crisis: What Every Trustee Must Know* (Association of Governing Boards of Universities and Colleges, 1982).

Enrollment projections are highly uncertain, depending as they do on a variety of hard-to-predict factors, and estimates cover a wide range.[84] On the optimistic end is the prediction that enrollments will actually *increase* over the period by 25 to 40 percent "on the assumption that long-term trends for increasing participation rates by youth will reassert themselves, with the 1970s set aside as a special period that is not consistent with more permanent and favorable tendencies." On the other end is the gloomy prediction that "the 1980s may well become the Dark Ages of higher education."[85] According to this view, enrollments could decline by 40 to 50 percent as the demographic effects are "compounded by the impact of a deterioration in the private rate of return in the labor market on investments in higher education."[86]

The prevailing view, however, is that the decline in undergraduate enrollments will be in the neighborhood of 15 percent, based on assumptions that various recruitment strategies (for example, increased retention of students and increased enrollments by nontraditional students, such as adults and foreigners) will offset about 40 percent of the decline expected from demographic factors alone.[87] Military recruitment would be largely unaffected by these strategies, because enrollment rates among the traditional male youth population would be expected to remain constant over the period.

In the event that these alternative strategies prove to be unsuccessful, however, higher education institutions worried about survival may attempt to increase the participation rate of traditional college-age youth,

84. Because higher education is not a neat and tidy activity with fixed boundaries and unchanging concepts and definitions, it is not surprising to find both inconsistencies and inconclusiveness among the several sources of statistical information on college students. Existing data are particularly weak in allowing one to track a given cohort of students, such as all eighteen-year-olds, through the transitions from high school to college freshmen, from freshmen to sophomores, and so on. And yet these are the data needed to understand the degree of competition between higher education and the military that a shrinking youth population will produce.

85. Carnegie Council on Policy Studies in Higher Education, *Three Thousand Futures: The Next Twenty Years of Higher Education* (Jossey-Bass, 1980), p. 34; and Joseph Froomkin, *Needed: A New Federal Policy for Higher Education*, no. 6 (George Washington University, Institute for Educational Leadership, 1978), p. 31.

86. This prospect cannot be completely dismissed since "a decrease of about one-third in [the] rate of return did occur from the mid-sixties to the mid-seventies." Carnegie Council, *Three Thousand Futures*, p. 34.

87. Breneman, *The Coming Enrollment Crisis*, pp. 7, 20.

perhaps by lowering admission requirements.[88] If postsecondary institutions were able to maintain the early 1980s *level* of enrollments among the male youth population, the qualified and available pool would shrink to about 556,000, and to meet expected requirements, other things held constant, the armed forces would have to attract two-thirds of them.

At the extreme, if all of the above—larger forces, stricter entry standards, and higher college participation rates—occurred together in the 1990s, the military services would have to attract about three out of every four male youths in the qualified and available male population. This would be a monumental challenge under any circumstances and probably insurmountable in a healthy economy.

Economic Recovery

The armed forces have traditionally experienced more difficulty in attracting higher-quality volunteers during periods of economic expansion and declining rates of unemployment (for example, 1976-79). Alternatively, when the labor market has slackened, as it did in 1973-74 and again in 1980-83, the number and quality of applicants have increased.

Thus it is to be expected that economic recovery would once again create a more competitive environment for the armed forces. If the administration's predictions of economic recovery hold, the overall unemployment rate will decline from 7.8 percent in 1984 to 5.7 percent in 1989, in which case the youth unemployment rate would be expected to decline by approximately 4.1 percentage points (20 percent) over the same period.[89] Taken by itself, an economic recovery of this magnitude

88. On a related point, it may seem surprising that in the face of predicted enrollment problems and a dramatic decline in veteran enrollments, the higher education community has not been actively supportive of proposals to reinstitute the GI bill. The ambivalence apparently stems from uncertainty about whether a new GI bill would be a substitute for existing student aid or a complement to it. Moreover, it is no secret that public and private institutions hold different views on the issue. If given a choice, for example, private institutions would tend to favor federal student aid programs if only because of their fear that a GI bill, which would be unlikely to offer large amounts of tuition support, would give their public counterparts a comparative advantage.

89. Overall unemployment estimates obtained from *Budget of the United States Government, FY 1985*, pp. 2-10, 2-11. Youth unemployment estimates based on Congressional Budget Office, "CBO's Method for Projecting the Recruitment and Retention of Enlisted Military Personnel," prepared by Joel N. Slackman (CBO, 1982), p. 11.

could be expected to result in a decline of as much as 10 percent in high-quality male volunteers by 1989.

The first signs that the economic recovery that started in fiscal year 1983 might be having an effect on military recruitment appeared in the statistics for the first quarter of fiscal 1984, which showed that the Army had 22 percent fewer applicants than during the same period the previous year. Although the Army exceeded its recruitment goals for the period and had large numbers of volunteers awaiting future entry, Army officials were concerned that "the first small piece of bad news . . . may be a harbinger."[90]

Options

Despite the successes of the early 1980s, the ability to man the nation's armed forces with enough qualified volunteers in the future cannot be taken for granted, given the uncertainties involved. As a matter of fact, if the volunteer system is to survive the challenges of the late 1980s and early 1990s, as described above, additional investment in the military payroll and recruiting budget may be necessary. Given the budgetary outlook, options for reducing the need for male volunteers or expanding the pool of qualified prospects will become more attractive. In any event, advocates of conscription, anticipating the futility and, indeed, the risk of attempting to maintain a system so sensitive to the vagaries of the marketplace and the budgetary process will continue to urge the nation to prepare for a return to some form of compulsory service.

Compensation and Recruitment

Daunting though the prospects might appear for attracting an increasing proportion of the male youth population, a large number of informed observers are optimistic that the armed forces will be able to meet their personnel needs for the foreseeable future. There are, however, differing views about the best way to ensure that outcome.

COMPETITIVE PAY. With the decision to end conscription in 1973, the military became another employer in the marketplace and, by implication, competitive pay levels became one of the linchpins of the

---

90. "Army Reports Downturn in '83 Recruiting," *Washington Post*, February 3, 1984.

all-volunteer force. That concept is no less important today; the need to keep military pay on a par with civilian pay has been underscored by a variety of groups. The Military Manpower Task Force, established by President Reagan in 1981 to review the military manpower situation, concluded that all military services except the Army would be likely to meet their future qualitative and quantitative recruitment goals. The Army, it was estimated, could overcome its shortages—expected to be relatively modest—by offering an appropriate combination of additional compensation incentives.[91] The Congressional Budget Office concluded that if military pay raises kept pace with those in the private sector, all services could be expected to meet congressionally imposed quality constraints through 1988, even though the proportion of male high school graduates would probably fall below the record-setting levels of the early 1980s.[92] Other manpower specialists were likewise optimistic: "Where a few years ago predictions of a return to peacetime conscription by the mid-1980s were common, more prevalent now is the view—which we share—that military strength and quality can be maintained at desired levels so long as the nation maintains its commitment to keeping military compensation, broadly construed, competitive with civilian compensation."[93]

The amount that would have to be invested in the military payroll to attract and retain enough qualified people is unclear. A lot would depend on the amount of quality considered necessary and on the state of the economy. For example, it has been estimated that to maintain the unusually high-quality profile of the early 1980s in the face of anticipated declines in the youth population and unemployment rates would require an increase in relative pay of at least 10 percent, which in fiscal 1984 terms would amount to about $4 billion.[94] It is possible that the same result could be achieved at a lower cost if future pay increases were applied selectively to skills that are in short supply.[95]

91. Military Manpower Task Force, "A Report to the President on the Status and Prospects of the All Volunteer Force," p. III-9.

92. Statement of Robert F. Hale, *Department of Defense Appropriations for Fiscal Year 1984*, Hearings before the Subcommittee on Manpower and Personnel of the Senate Armed Services Committee, 98 Cong. 1 sess. (GPO, 1984), pt. 3, p. 1650.

93. Richard L. Fernendez and James R. Hosek, "Active Enlisted Supply: Prospects and Policy Options," paper prepared for a conference on "The AVF After a Decade: Retrospect and Prospect," U.S. Naval Academy, November 1983, p. 2.

94. Ibid., p. 16.

95. See Martin Binkin and Irene Kyriakopoulos, *Paying the Modern Military* (Brookings Institution, 1981); and Statement of Robert F. Hale.

The nation's commitment to maintaining competitive pay levels, however, appears fragile. Many oppose large increases in military compensation on the grounds that payroll costs have already imposed too large a burden on the defense budget. Others contend that military manpower problems are not related solely to compensation levels and that pay increases would not be sufficient to resolve contemporary problems, particularly those related to social composition and organizational cohesiveness. Still others oppose large increases on the grounds of efficiency, arguing that many of today's problems are largely a result of outmoded manpower policies.

Even the strong pro-defense Reagan administration failed to live up to early expectations that pay for members of the armed forces would be a priority issue and, at the least, would keep pace with private-sector pay. Substantial increases were granted in the first year of the administration, accompanied by strong hints that more would be coming. But in 1982, plagued by economic problems and buoyed by recruitment successes, Reagan capped military pay raises for fiscal year 1983 at 4 percent—about one-half of the increase necessary to maintain "comparability"—and proposed to freeze military pay for fiscal 1984, while requesting a defense budget 11 percent larger than the previous year. The Congress, nevertheless, granted a raise of 4 percent, effective January 1, 1984, still somewhat smaller than the comparable civilian increase (the Professional, Administrative, Technical, and Clerical Index increased by 7.4 percent and the Employment Cost Index rose by 5.6 percent during the year ending March 1983). Although the armed forces met short-term manning goals, the longer-term impact remained unclear. Some feared that a "feast-or-famine" cycle of military pay increases would eventually lead to manpower problems and, for some observers at least, fueled the contention that it is imprudent to link a recruitment system so closely to pay incentives.

EDUCATIONAL BENEFITS. Apart from pay, educational benefits are widely viewed as one of the most important tangible incentives for attracting military volunteers. In fact, critics of the perceived socioeconomic imbalance in the armed forces feel that a greater emphasis on educational benefits and less on pay would motivate the enlistment of middle-class, college-bound youth—traditionally the most difficult to attract to military service.

But virtually every economic assessment of alternative recruitment incentives has concluded that, if the objective is to attract a given additional number of highly qualified volunteers, educational benefits are not the incentive of choice.[96] This is largely because most broad educational benefit programs share a disadvantage with many across-the-board approaches: since the benefits are offered to and inevitably used by some service members who would have been attracted without them, costs are larger than necessary. In addition, once vested, these benefits provide an incentive to quit the military. As more service members decide to leave the military, additional volunteers must be recruited to replace them, thereby tending to offset the recruitment response that the educational benefit programs are designed to stimulate.

Despite the strong opposition of the administration and the ambivalence of military leaders, veterans' groups, and the higher education community, efforts to secure a new GI bill nonetheless persist. Legislation tacked onto the 1985 defense authorization bill by Representative G. V. (Sonny) Montgomery, Democrat of Mississippi, and passed by the House in early 1984 would replace VEAP with a noncontributory GI bill. Additional incentives would attract volunteers with critical skills and discourage people from leaving the service to use their benefits. The Senate then passed a more modest version, sponsored by Senator John Glenn, Democrat of Ohio, that would complement rather than replace VEAP. It would require two-year enlistees to take a large cut in pay in order to receive sizable educational benefits after leaving the service; it would be restricted to a four-year test involving up to 12,500 recruits a year.[97] The final details of a new educational benefits program will depend on compromises struck in conference committee.

RECRUITING RESOURCES. A growing body of opinion holds that additional recruiting resources would be more efficient than increases in either financial or educational incentives to stave off recruitment shortfalls. The Congressional Budget Office, for example, estimated in 1982 that additional recruiters in the field would produce high-quality male volunteers (those with a high school degree and above-average aptitude) for the Army at a marginal cost of $22,000 per recruit, compared with about $200,000 for an across-the-board GI bill and $35,000 for an enlistment bonus program.[98] While current estimates of recruiter elas-

96. An excellent analysis of the issue can be found in CBO, *Improving Military Educational Benefits*.

97. Martha Lynn Craver, "Conferees Meeting on Authorization Bill Issues," *Navy Times*, July 2, 1984.

98. CBO, *Improving Military Educational Benefits*, p. 50.

ticity vary, it is generally concluded that a 10 percent increase in the number of recruiters would produce at least a 5 percent increase in the number of enlistees. There is less of a consensus, however, on the range over which this estimate might be appropriate. "Diminishing returns are inevitable," according to one study, "but we have not reached the point where investment in greater numbers of recruiters is uneconomic." Based on the estimate that "a 20 percent decline in the youth population could be substantially or completely offset by a proportionate increase in recruiting resources," proponents of this approach conclude that the upcoming decline in the youth population may not be as threatening to the volunteer concept as commonly thought.[99]

Manpower Management

In addition to competitive pay levels, efficiency in manpower management had been an important premise of the architects of the volunteer concept. The strongest supporters of voluntary recruitment lay many of the problems that plagued the system in the 1970s at the doorstep of the military's top managers, who were charged with being less than enthusiastic about breaking with traditional—but anachronistic—personnel practices.[100]

During three decades of practically continuous conscription the armed forces managed their human resources within the confines of a unique system largely unaffected by the rules of the American marketplace. With a virtually endless reservoir of recruits, the military was under little pressure to use people efficiently. With the adoption of the volunteer system, however, the "free good" element in military manpower disappeared, and as the defense budget more accurately reflected the true marginal costs of military manpower, personnel policies were more closely scrutinized.

As early as 1973 an assessment of the prospects for success concluded that the all-volunteer force "is likely to prove a feasible proposition, *if* timely measures are taken to reevaluate manpower requirements and

99. Gary R. Nelson, "The Supply and Quality of First-Term Enlistees under the All-Volunteer Force," prepared for a conference on "The AVF after a Decade: Retrospect and Prospect," U.S. Naval Academy, November 1983, pp. 43, 49.

100. See Gus C. Lee and Geoffrey Y. Parker, *Ending the Draft: The Story of the All Volunteer Force*, FR-PO-77-1 (Alexandria, Va.: Human Resources Research Organization, 1977), pp. 208-14.

standards and to deal with foreseeable recruiting shortfalls."[101] A fresh examination was needed, it was argued, of the role of women; the potential for civilian substitution; the educational, mental, and physical standards for enlistment; the youth-experience mix in the armed forces; and the possibility of attracting postsecondary students—all issues designed to reassess the demand for and the supply of *male* volunteers.

Several things were done during the 1970s to reduce the requirement for new male recruits: the size of the forces was modestly cut; the roles of women in uniform and of federal civilians were expanded; contracts were let with the private sector for certain services previously provided by military troops; and more personnel were retained beyond the first enlistment period. The net effect was to reduce the average annual intake of male recruits from 364,000 during the first several years of the volunteer force to just over 280,000 in the early 1980s. The extent to which the need for male recruits can be further trimmed by manipulating these policy variables remains open to debate.

CIVILIAN SUBSTITUTION. The ground rules that govern the relative numbers of military and civilian employees in the armed forces are imprecise, and the rationale underlying the determination of the current composition is unclear. Whether combat forces—for example, Army or Marine Corps infantrymen, naval destroyer crews, and Air Force strategic bomber crews—should be military or civilian is obviously not at issue. And few would doubt that those who directly support the combat forces and are expected to operate in a combat zone should be uniformed personnel.

Even when agreement is reached on this obvious point—that "combat forces" should be composed of military personnel—a question remains: what constitutes "combat forces?" The distinctions are not as sharp as they appear. Must crews flying and servicing airlift aircraft similar in configuration to those used commercially, such as the C-5, be military? Must naval support ships, such as oilers and tenders, be manned by naval personnel? In fact, some civilian contractor employees routinely deploy with the combat fleet. And drawing the line between military and civilian personnel combat support functions becomes more difficult when it is recalled that U.S. combat forces currently deployed rely on foreign national civilians for certain forms of support.

101. Martin Binkin and John D. Johnston, *All-Volunteer Armed Forces: Progress, Problems, and Prospects*, prepared for the Senate Armed Services Committee, 93 Cong. 1 sess. (GPO, 1973), especially chap. 4.

Because so much depends on how combat is defined and on military judgment, the task of determining which jobs require a military incumbent would be difficult even if data on individual jobs were available. By rough estimate, approximately 80 percent of all enlisted positions are deployed overseas in peacetime, earmarked for deployment in wartime, or set aside for rotation purposes to ensure that military personnel are not required to spend a disproportionate share of their time in deployed billets. The question of how many of the roughly 300,000 remaining jobs could and should be filled by civilians deserves further analysis.[102]

REDUCED TURNOVER. The possibilities for developing a more experienced force also warrant additional investigation. The retention of a larger proportion of military personnel beyond a first enlistment period would not only reduce turnover and hence the requirement for new recruits, but it would also provide an effective corps of specialists and technicians more closely matched to the technological needs of the modern military establishment.

The appropriate mix of career and first-term members should be determined by a cost-effectiveness test, but it is important to recognize that the ability to field more seasoned forces is circumscribed first by extant military personnel policies, the centerpiece of which is the promotion system, and second by the military compensation system, which has emphasized rank rather than occupation, job setting, or investment in training. To realize the full potential that a more experienced military establishment could provide would require a restructuring of both.[103]

EXPANDED ROLE FOR WOMEN. The possibilities for further expanding participation by women also deserve close scrutiny. It is widely acknowledged that women were the saving grace of the volunteer concept during the 1970s. In 1972, when the decision was made to increase the proportion of women in the military, some 45,000 women constituted 1.9 percent of all active-duty military personnel; of these women, the vast majority (91 percent) held traditionally female jobs, such as medical

---

102. For a fuller discussion of the potential for civilian substitution and of the domestic and bureaucratic politics involved, see Martin Binkin with Herschel Kanter and Rolf H. Clark, *Shaping the Defense Civilian Work Force: Economics, Politics, and National Security* (Brookings Institution, 1978).

103. See Martin Binkin and Irene Kyriakopoulos, *Youth or Experience? Manning the Modern Military* (Brookings Institution, 1979); and Binkin and Kyriakopoulos, *Paying the Modern Military*.

and dental specialists or clerical workers. By contrast, in 1983 over 196,000 women constituted about 9.3 percent of the total force, and 45 percent of them were assigned to nontraditional jobs.[104]

In the late 1970s the Carter administration had envisioned a continued moderate rate of growth that would result in over 265,000 women in the military by fiscal 1986. But with the change of administration in 1981, the expansion plans were tabled, pending a review of the impact of women on force readiness.[105] This was justified by the Pentagon on the grounds that "the increase [during the 1970s] was spurred primarily by social pressures for equal opportunity with particular emphasis on utilization of women in nontraditional skills . . . [and] little effort was made during this period to empirically determine the best way to utilize women based on skill, mission, and readiness requirements."[106] Following internal reviews, the goals were revised downward. According to the projections available in 1984, by fiscal year 1986 there will be about 216,000 women in the military, approximately 20,000 more than in fiscal year 1983, but some 50,000 short of the number envisioned by the Carter administration. A breakdown by service is shown below:[107]

| Service | Fiscal 1986 goals | |
	Carter	Reagan
Army	99,000	80,900
Navy	53,700	51,400
Air Force	103,200	74,000
Marine Corps	9,600	9,500
Total	265,500	215,800

The downward revision in the Army's goals for women followed the findings of the Women in the Army Policy Review Group. Assuming that soldiers filling particular jobs might find themselves in direct combat in fluid wartime situations, this group concluded that 61 military occu-

104. Martin Binkin and Mark J. Eitelberg, "Women and Minorities in the All-Volunteer Force," paper prepared for a conference on "The All-Volunteer Force after a Decade: Retrospect and Prospect," U.S. Naval Academy, November 1983, tables 9 and 11.

105. Holm, *Women in the Military,* pp. 380-88.

106. U.S. Department of Defense, Office of the Assistant Secretary of Defense for Manpower, Reserve Affairs, and Logistics, *Military Women in the Department of Defense* (DOD, 1983), p. 1.

107. Carter administration goals appear in Holm, *Women in the Military,* p. 381. Reagan administration goals provided by Office of the Assistant Secretary of Defense for Manpower, Reserve Affairs, and Logistics.

pations (including carpenters and plumbers), accounting for over 300,000 jobs, should be closed to women. Included in the list were 23 occupations that previously had been open to them. Subsequently, under pressure from the Pentagon's civilian leadership, the Army decided that only 49 of 351 career fields would be closed.[108]

Critics claim the revised goals are arbitrary and are merely elements of a "hidden agenda" by the armed forces to return to the draft.[109] Some have questioned the rationale underlying the Army's combat exclusion policy, claiming that it is needlessly restrictive to close jobs to women based on proximity to the battlefield. Their principal argument is that in an age of long-range precision-guided weapons casualties will not be restricted to the front areas. While most do not argue against the exclusion of women from jobs that are indisputably combat (such as infantryman or tank driver), they object to policies that bar women from jobs based on probability estimates of direct physical contact with the enemy or risk of capture.

The rationale underlying the even larger reduction in the Air Force goal for fiscal 1987 is more difficult to pin down. Presumably the Air Force forecast considers the following factors: "propensity of women to enlist in the Air Force, propensity of women to enlist in a particular skill, and a projection of the number of women who will qualify by aptitude and physically (including strength measurement) in each skill."[110] But how these factors are calculated and how they translate into specific goals has not been made public. Major General Jeanne Holm, the first woman to achieve that rank in the Air Force and now retired from active duty, has expressed a healthy measure of skepticism:

Air Force planners . . . have worried that if the Army were permitted to reduce its intake of women in the coming years, the Air Force could be required to take more than its "fair share" to meet overall DOD female strength requirements. They are well aware that their service is especially vulnerable in this respect because its capacity to absorb women without infringing on combat policies is, for all practical purposes, unlimited. The Air Force is hard pressed, therefore, to come up with any rationale for *not* using more women that will

108. U.S. Department of the Army, Office of the Deputy Chief of Staff for Personnel, *Women in the Army Policy Review* (DOA, 1982), pp. 5-5, 5-6; and News Release no. 522-83, U.S. Department of Defense, Office of the Assistant Secretary, October 20, 1983.

109. Holm, *Women in the Military*, p. 385.

110. Memorandum, "Methodology for Determining Number of Enlisted Women," Office of the Assistant Secretary of Defense for Manpower, Reserve Affairs, and Logistics, March 17, 1983.

withstand objective analysis. Statements of concern about their impact on readiness and having "too many" women in traditional fields, etc., are thinly veiled attempts to give legitimacy to what is in fact an arbitrary decision on the part of Air Force planners to hold down the numbers of women.[111]

At bottom, the principal issue involving women and the military is the extent to which remaining laws and policies that constrain further expansion are justified by valid national security concerns or instead are anchored to sexual stereotypes of an earlier era. The future utilization of women—and perhaps the future of the volunteer concept—will depend on the resolution of this issue.

LARGER RECRUITMENT MARKET. The qualified and available male population, as defined earlier, excluded certain categories of individuals. Changes in recruitment policies and entry standards could bring some of these categories into the supply pool, thus increasing the number of potential volunteers.

Since college students have typically not shown interest in serving in the enlisted ranks, the armed forces understandably have dedicated few recruiting resources to the campus market. Even in the banner recruitment year of 1983, when an unprecedented proportion of Army recruits were high school graduates, fewer than one out of ten volunteers had any postsecondary education and only 6 percent had completed at least two years (see table 3). Although it is unreasonable to expect that the military services could attract large numbers of graduates of four-year colleges and universities into the enlisted force, it is appropriate to consider the extent to which they might attract graduates of two-year junior or community college programs. An assessment is difficult since so little is known about either the number of students involved or their characteristics and propensities.

It has been conservatively estimated that as of 1980 over 1 million males in the age range acceptable to the armed forces were enrolled in two-year colleges. A large majority of these students could be expected to meet the military's entrance requirements, but the extent to which their addition to the ranks would improve the overall quality of the force is unknown. The limited and somewhat dated information that is available confirms the self-evident: by and large, students in two-year college programs tend to have poorer credentials than their counterparts in four-year colleges but better than their contemporaries in the military and civilian work force. But the data were too sparse to warrant anything

111. Holm, *Women in the Military*, p. 392.

stronger than the suggestion "that there is a concentrated market of potential recruits who appear to meet enlistment standards."[112]

On the question of market penetrability, the conclusion was equally tentative: "(a) students in two-year colleges have not been a major source of accessions in the past, (b) few freshmen in two-year colleges appear to consider military service as an occupational option, (c) students in two-year colleges often change their educational and occupational plans, and (d) present research has not adequately addressed the penetrability of the two-year college market."[113]

A bill introduced in the Ninety-eighth Congress by Representative Charles E. Bennett, Democrat of Florida, takes a different approach to the same issue. Under the terms of the bill, "community colleges and technical institutes would provide high school graduates technical training leading to an associate degree or technical certificate, simultaneously with the preparation of such high school graduates for military service in a pay grade commensurate with their training."[114] This program, according to its sponsor, could lead to savings of up to $10 billion in training costs by 1987, an estimate that the Congressional Budget Office was unable to substantiate.[115]

If the past is any guide, however, the armed forces would be hesitant to support increased penetration of the two-year college market. The services have traditionally opposed policies that would perturb their closed personnel system, in which all workers are hired at the entry level, at the bottom of a hierarchical pyramid, and vacancies are normally filled internally by promotions. Although several programs exist that allow people to enter at higher grades ("lateral entries") and that allow accelerated promotions, they have been limited in scope. The services believe that awarding advanced rank to new entrants disrupts the normal promotion flow and creates morale problems among those not receiving

112. Richard J. Shavelson, Gus W. Haggstrom, and John D. Winkler, *Potential for Military Recruiting from Two-Year Colleges and Post-Secondary Vocational Schools,* N-1946-MRAL, prepared for the Office of the Assistant Secretary of Defense for Manpower, Reserve Affairs, and Logistics (Santa Monica: Rand Corp., 1983), p. 22.

113. Ibid., p. 38.

114. H. R. 1937, Skilled Enlisted Reserve Training Act.

115. For a discussion of the bill, see *Congressional Record,* daily edition (March 9, 1983), p. H1084. The CBO was quite skeptical: "Savings averaging $10 billion per year over five years seem excessive in the light of the fact that DOD plans to spend less than that on current technical training programs in fiscal year 1984." Enclosure to letter from Rudolph G. Penner, director, Congressional Budget Office, to Representative Les Aspin, Chairman, Military Personnel and Compensation Subcommittee, House Committee on Armed Services, October 26, 1983.

the premium. Moreover, it is argued that bringing in new people at higher entry ranks ignores the traditional view that military leadership is a function of maturity, as well as skill attainment. One possible way around these concerns would be to loosen the current link between rank and pay grade and tie the latter more closely to the occupation, the job setting, the investment in training, and alternative job opportunities in the civilian economy.[116] In that way, the services could vary entry pay without disturbing the rank structure and perhaps attract a larger share of the college market.

ADJUSTED QUALITY STANDARDS. Another approach for expanding the supply of prospective male volunteers, which has been used in the past, is to adjust educational and test score entry requirements.[117] Actually, specifications concerning the quality mix of recruits are arbitrary since there are no hard-and-fast rules for judging how smart or how well-educated individuals must be to function effectively in the armed forces. According to a former Pentagon manpower official:

As a manpower manager I would like to be able to measure the quality of personnel with confidence and to tie that measurement closely and predictably to effective job performance. Unfortunately our capacity to measure individual attributes is imperfect; and our capacity to relate those attributes to on-the-job performance is rudimentary.[118]

Although the armed forces have established minimum educational and aptitude standards for entry into the military and into specific skill training courses, the procedures are not sufficiently refined to permit the individual services to specify the mix of educational and aptitude attributes that would maximize effectiveness. It is no secret, nor is it particularly surprising, that in the absence of this capability the services seek to attract as many high school graduates with above-average aptitude as possible.

Several attempts have been made to define the military's personnel quality needs. In 1973 Secretary of Defense Elliot L. Richardson suggested that too much quality could be counterproductive:

Overall, the learning capacity of new entries is adequate in meeting job

---

116. The benefits of this approach are discussed in Binkin and Kyriakopoulos, *Paying the Modern Military*.

117. A comprehensive historical review of the application of military standards can be found in Mark J. Eitelberg and others, *Screening for Service: Aptitude and Education Criteria for Military Entry* (Alexandria, Va.: Human Resources Research Organization, 1983).

118. Robert B. Pirie, Jr., "Enlistment Test Scores: What Do They Really Measure?" *Defense 80* (June 1980), pp. 10-13.

requirements when the proportion of Mental Group IV personnel does not exceed about 22 percent. Conversely, when the overall proportion of Mental Group IV personnel falls below 15 percent, there is a tendency toward many people being under-challenged by their job assignments.[119]

In 1980, in response to the sharp decline in recruit quality, Congress established ceilings on the proportion of recruits in the lowest aptitude category. In fiscal 1981 not more than 25 percent of the recruits for all military services could be from personnel scoring between the tenth and thirtieth percentiles on the entrance examination. For fiscal year 1982 each individual service could not exceed the 25 percent maximum, and the ceiling was lowered to 20 percent for fiscal year 1983 and beyond.[120] Upper limits were also placed on high school dropouts (Army only) in fiscal 1981 and succeeding years: no more than 35 percent of the Army's male recruits could be nongraduates.[121] Although lacking an analytical foundation of their own, the congressional constraints were subsequently supported by an independent scholar, who concluded that the quotas established by Congress approximated the "optimal levels" indicated by an analysis of Army performance.[122]

A study group convened in 1981 by the Atlantic Council of the United States to examine the issue of military service also attempted to define an appropriate quality mix, recommending that at least 65 percent of recruits have a high school diploma, at least half score at or above the fiftieth percentile on the standardized entry test, and no more than 25 percent score in the lowest aptitude category (IV). These quotas, the group contended, would "avoid a gross unrepresentativeness of the educational background and mental capacity of the population."[123]

The arbitrariness of such quotas has been criticized by both past and present Pentagon manpower officials. Dissenting from the Atlantic

119. "The All-Volunteer Force and the End of the Draft," A Special Report of Secretary of Defense Elliot L. Richardson (1973), p. 13.

120. Department of Defense Authorization Act, 1981, sec. 302, 94 Stat. 1082.

121. Ibid.; 1982, sec. 402, 95 Stat. 1104; 1983, sec. 403, 96 Stat. 725; 1984, sec. 402, 97 Stat. 629.

122. David J. Armor, *Enlistment Standards in the Army,* P-6701 (Santa Monica: Rand Corp., 1981), p. 12.

123. J. Allen Hovey, Jr., "The Policy Paper: Toward a Consensus on Military Service," in Goodpaster, Elliott, and Hovey, eds., *Toward a Consensus on Military Service,* p. 299. It is estimated that among American youth aged eighteen to twenty-three 74 percent would have a high school diploma, 50 percent would have an AFQT score at or above the fiftieth percentile, and 23 percent would fall in category IV. Derived from data provided by Defense Manpower Data Center.

Council group recommendation, Robert B. Pirie, Jr., the top defense manpower official in the Carter administration, contended that "nobody knows whether the minimums recommended are right, necessary, feasible or appropriate."[124] His successor in the Reagan administration, Lawrence J. Korb, took a similar position:

The recommended quality standards are arbitrary and based on a representativeness policy. . . . The paper suggests floors which almost perfectly match the aptitude in the general society. We do not believe that those floors are appropriate for several reasons:

—The enlisted force is primarily "blue collar" in nature. Thus it is composed of jobs which require a smaller proportion of individuals in the upper-ability ranges.

—The representativeness standard is inappropriate, military need should govern.

—The costs to achieve those standards would be prohibitive and there would be substantial risk they could not be achieved, notwithstanding the new proposals for short term enlistments made in the paper.

—Any representative comparison should be made against the entire force, officer and enlisted.

—Each Service has different jobs to be performed; those jobs translate into different percentages of mental categories needed.[125]

Substantial controversy thus surrounds the quality question. As matters stand, there is no agreed-upon method for estimating an optimal, minimal, or otherwise appropriate distribution of educational and aptitude attainment among military recruits. Until a better understanding of this issue is provided by further research, the possibility of enlarging the pool of eligibles by adjusting entry standards, as has been done so often in the past, should not be ruled out.

Alternatives to the All-Volunteer Force

If the force of events—military, financial, political, or social—compels the nation to rethink its military manpower procurement policy, alternatives to voluntary recruitment will have to be considered. The possibilities are abundant, ranging from a narrow *selective* service program, in which some portion of the eligible population serves in the armed forces, to broad *national* service, in which virtually everyone serves in either a military or a civilian capacity.

124. Ibid., p. 308.
125. Ibid., note on p. 300.

MILITARY CONSCRIPTION. At one extreme, the nation could pick up where it left off in 1973 by resurrecting a lottery draft with few exemptions, deferments, or excusals. While this option would ensure that the armed forces could maintain their authorized strengths, the extent to which it would affect recruit quality, social balance, or reserve manning would depend on the number of inductees relative to the number of volunteers and the number of youth in the eligible population. If only a small proportion of the Army's recruit needs were to be met through conscription, for example, the qualitative and demographic characteristics of the recruit population would continue to be shaped largely by the attributes of volunteers; moreover, the small number to be drafted would put relatively little pressure on youth to join the reserves. This ratio would change if volunteers were somehow discouraged, say, by lowering recruit pay or if the supply of eligible volunteers were somehow reduced, say, by raising enlistment standards.

The ratio of draftees to volunteers would also be affected by changes in the size of the Army. If, for example, Army enlisted strength were expanded by 100,000, the average annual requirement for new male recruits could be expect to grow from about 115,000 to about 130,000. If the Army were able to attract, say, the same number of volunteers with the same qualifications that characterized fiscal 1981 recruitment, the shortfall would be at most 50,000. If this were to be made up through a no-exemption, no-deferment lottery draft yielding a cross section of those youth eligible for military service under 1981 enlistment standards, it is estimated that 83 percent of the Army's recruits would have a high school diploma (compared with 78 percent in 1981), 18 percent would be in the lowest aptitude category (compared with 32 percent in 1981), and 17 percent would be black (compared with 26 percent in 1981).[126] Reserve recruitment would also be expected to improve, if only modestly. Finally, a draft would do little to fulfill the military's needs for experienced specialists and technicians; in fact, if draftees were less likely than volunteers to reenlist, conscription could be counterproductive in coping with the demands of high technology.

To those concerned more about the nation's mobilization capabilities than about active force manning, conscription confined to the reserves makes more sense. Proposals to draft youth into selected reserve units have been proposed, as have suggestions to conscript only for the

126. See Binkin, Eitelberg, and others, *Blacks and the Military*, p. 146.

Individual Ready Reserve.[127] As in the case of a draft for the active forces, however, a reserve draft would also necessarily be selective.[128]

Given the contemporary social and political settings, the chances of returning to a peacetime military draft must be regarded as slim. That a majority of the American people support conscription has been confirmed by virtually every public opinion poll taken in recent years. Yet, as in other national issues, the views of affected interest groups—in this case the younger generation—must be considered. As the Vietnam era illustrated, the alienation of American youth exacts a large and enduring toll on society. Thus national leaders are wary of reawakening campus activism that has been relatively dormant since the last chorus of "Hell no, we won't go!" By some accounts, the current generation is less idealistic and more inward looking than the protest generation of the 1960s, but just as likely to oppose compulsory military service.[129]

The scenario that would galvanize their support for peacetime conscription is difficult to predict, and the willingness of the national leadership to proceed without that support is equally unclear. It is tempting to believe that the current generation of young Americans would respond in the face of a distinct danger, but there is no clear conception of just what would constitute such a threat. It is doubtful that the cold war rhetoric that sustained peacetime conscription without major dissent during the 1950s and early 1960s would be sufficient today; indeed, there is widespread agreement that the political and social costs of resuming a draft merely to alleviate modest shortfalls in quantity or quality or to redress the social imbalance of today's volunteer forces are prohibitive. These costs would lessen if the manning problems of the late 1970s were revisited or, of course, if a major international crisis developed. Even then, the disposition of conscientious objectors (COs) would have to be considered. This has become a particularly worrisome problem since conscientious objection was liberalized by the Supreme

127. An assessment of these proposals and an excellent overall treatment of alternatives to all-volunteer forces can be found in James L. Lacy, "Obligatory Service: The Fundamental and Secondary Choices," in Goodpaster, Elliott, and Hovey, eds., *Toward a Consensus on Military Service*, pp. 200-34.

128. Unless, of course, something like universal military training is adopted. But this possibility is usually dismissed on the grounds that having literally millions of troops who had received only basic training would not serve a useful military purpose.

129. For a profile of the current generation of college students, see Arthur Levine, *When Dreams and Heroes Died: A Portrait of Today's College Student*, prepared for the Carnegie Council on Policy Studies in Higher Education (Jossey-Bass, 1980).

Court in the 1960s. As matters stand, CO status is more a matter of assertion than of demonstration; this unprecedented legitimacy would be expected to swell the ranks of those who would seek CO status in a peacetime draft situation.[130]

NATIONAL SERVICE. These concerns have prompted some advocates of conscription to propose compulsory options that would involve a larger proportion of the nation's youth and, in some cases, accommodate with minimum divisiveness those who would seek CO status. A program that would require all qualified youth to serve their country in one capacity or another is attractive not only to those interested in improving the state of the nation's military preparedness but also to those with broader interests in improving American society. Thus the issue has been joined by veterans of the Peace Corps and VISTA programs of the 1960s, who see a new opportunity to rekindle the spirit reflected in John F. Kennedy's dictum: "Ask not what your country can do for you—ask what you can do for your country."[131]

The broad concept of national service is instinctively appealing and appears to enjoy the widespread support of many elements of American society.[132] But the gulf between a broad concept and a specific program is wide: the social, political, and economic hurdles are formidable. First, the cost of a comprehensive national service program has been placed at up to $24 billion a year.[133] Second, some worry that 3.5 to 4 million

130. See James L. Lacy, "Military Manpower: The American Experience and the Enduring Debate," in Goodpaster, Elliott, and Hovey, eds., *Toward a Consensus on Military Service*, pp. 40-41. There is little basis for estimating the numbers who would request CO exemption, but in contrast to an estimated 72,000 claims in all of World War II, more than 121,000 young men applied for CO status in fiscal year 1971 alone. Kenneth J. Coffey, *Strategic Implications of the All-Volunteer Force* (University of North Carolina Press, 1979), p. 8.

131. Jacqueline Grennan Wexler and Harris Wofford, both of whom had been involved in early discussions of plans for national service in the mid-1960s while working together in the Peace Corps, cochaired the Committee for the Study of National Service established in 1977. The report to the committee, which recommended that the nation "move toward universal service by stages and by incentives but without compulsion," was published as *Youth and the Needs of the Nation*, report of the Committee for the Study of National Service (Washington, D.C.: Potomac Institute, 1979).

132. For example, a Gallup poll in 1981 reported that 71 percent of the American people favored "requiring all young men to give one year of service to the nation—either in the military forces or in non-military work here or abroad, such as work in hospitals or with elderly people." Fifty-four percent supported the same proposition for young women. *The Gallup Report*, no. 189 (June 1981), p. 18.

133. Congressional Budget Office, *National Service Programs and Their Effects on Military Manpower and Civilian Youth Problems* (CBO, January 1978), p. 84.

youths (males and females) could not be productively employed in public service for one year. Third, a national service draft of this scope might well displace some workers in the labor force. Fourth, compulsory national service could well fail a test of constitutionality. Accordingly, a number of variations of national service have been proposed, differing in terms of scope, level of participation, orientation, and cost.[134]

Advocates of *voluntary* national service envisage a program that would provide "universality of opportunity" to all American youths for a "full-time experience that permits them to learn about the world of work, establish a creditable work record, and earn financial support for further education and training." The architects of this proposal advocate a gradual buildup, with the number of participants reaching 100,000 by the end of the first year and growing to about 1 million by the end of the third year. Annual costs ultimately would reach $8 billion to $10 billion (in 1981 dollars), depending on the extent to which educational fellowships would be provided to those who serve. Although this plan was designed specifically as a civilian youth service program that "should exist independently of the military establishment," its proponents contend that "if the government expressed its trust in young people by inviting them to serve for a period in voluntary national service, before long young people would come to appreciate the government's trust by enlisting in the military in sufficient numbers to obviate the need for a draft."[135]

A version of voluntary national service proposed by Charles Moskos, on the other hand, gives greater priority to meeting military manpower needs without reliance on conscription or on cash inducements for recruits. An emphasis on the latter, according to Moskos, has filled the armed forces with too many deprived youths, many with dependents, who view the military in terms of an occupation rather than a calling. His proposal, designed to provide the armed forces with "the analogue of the peacetime draftee in the all-volunteer context," would (1) link federal aid for higher education to a program of voluntary national service to include military reserve duty or civilian work; (2) introduce a GI bill along the lines of the post–World War II version; and (3) construct a two-track military personnel and compensation system that differen-

---

134. These variations are discussed in Michael W. Sherraden and Donald J. Eberly, eds., *National Service: Social, Economic and Military Impacts* (Pergamon Press, 1982); and Lacy, "Obligatory Service."

135. Sherraden and Eberly, *National Service*, pp. 104-06, 108-09.

tiates between a short-term volunteer and one who makes a long-term commitment. This approach, it is contended, would attract to the armed forces middle-class college-bound youth "who would find a temporary diversion from the world of school or work tolerable, and perhaps even welcome."[136]

Other observers are skeptical that a completely voluntary system would satisfy the armed forces' needs, but acknowledge the necessity to provide American youth with alternatives to military service. Thus *selective* national service has emerged as a compromise between voluntary and compulsory schemes and between military and civilian orientation. Several versions that have been proposed share some common characteristics:

—Acceptable civilian service would have to be in an approved field or activity, almost always in the delivery of social service;

—Those electing this nonmilitary service would have to make the election before they received an induction notice, commonly at the time of initial draft registration (in some versions, however, the individual may delay actual commencement of service for up to four years);

—Failure to elect civilian service subjects the individual to liability to induction by random lottery for an active tour of military duty; failure to satisfactorily complete such service subjects the individual to another period of lottery exposure;

—Satisfactory completion of service is not cause for a draft exemption per se, but those who have served are placed low enough in the order of call of any future draft, in peacetime and in war, to make it unlikely they will be called.[137]

One version of a selective national service proposal was the National Service Act introduced in 1979 by Representative Paul N. (Pete) Mc-Closkey, Republican of California. Under its terms, registrants would have the following options: (1) volunteer for two years of active military service; (2) volunteer for six months of active military service followed by 5½ years of reserve military service; (3) volunteer for one year of service in a civilian capacity; or (4) be placed in a lottery pool in which they would be vulnerable for six years to conscription into the armed forces, where, if inducted, they would serve two years on active duty

136. Moskos, "Social Considerations of the All-Volunteer Force," pp. 145-46, 150. Also see Moskos, "Making the All-Volunteer Force Work: A National Service Approach," *Foreign Affairs*, vol. 60 (Fall 1981), pp. 17-34.

137. Lacy, "Obligatory Service," pp. 225-26.

and four years in the reserves. All volunteers would be allowed to defer service until the age of twenty-three, and those electing two years of military service would be entitled to four years of educational benefits at the same rate provided to Vietnam-era veterans, adjusted for the cost of living since that time. Military conscripts would be entitled to two years of educational benefits.[138]

The issue, however, has not been high on the congressional priority list. Although legislation to create a select commission to study *voluntary* national service, introduced in 1981 by Representative Leon E. Panetta, Democrat of California, was approved by the House Committee on Education and Labor, the proposal was not taken up on the floor. A similar bill, reintroduced by the congressman in 1983, again cleared the committee, but was defeated on the floor, 245 to 179.[139] Meanwhile, Senator Paul Tsongas, Democrat of Massachusetts, introduced a related bill on the Senate side.[140] Practically speaking, however, the little interest that Congress had shown in national service all but disappeared as the military manpower situation improved and is unlikely to be revived unless peacetime conscription again receives serious consideration.

Summary: The Next Decade

In November 1983 Secretary of Defense Caspar W. Weinberger proclaimed that the volunteer force was no longer experimental. "We know now that an all-volunteer force can succeed," he said, "and we know what it takes to make it succeed. We need only the will, the perseverance—and the commitment to quality."[141] This unbridled opti-

138. Details of this proposal are discussed in Congressional Budget Office, *Costs of the National Service Act (H.R. 2206): A Technical Analysis,* prepared by Joel N. Slackman (CBO, 1980); Carnegie Council on Policy Studies in Higher Education, *Giving Youth a Better Chance: Options for Education, Work, and Service* (Jossey-Bass, 1979), pp. 275-76; and Sherraden and Eberly, *National Service,* pp. 90-92. The last reference includes a discussion of the Cavanaugh plan, a version of selective national service that would, like the McCloskey plan, subject to a lottery those who did not volunteer for military or civilian service, but would require those inducted to serve in either a military or civilian position.

139. H.R. 1264, Select Commission on Voluntary Service Opportunities Act of 1982. For floor discussion of the bill, see *Congressional Record,* daily edition (November 16, 1983), pp. H10026-31. Voting results appear in *Congressional Record,* daily edition (November 17, 1983), p. H10099.

140. S. 1896, Select Commission on Voluntary Opportunities Act of 1983.

141. "Weinberger Calls AVF 'Huge Success,' " *Army Times,* November 21, 1983.

mism, understandable as it is given the successes during his tenure, may be premature. The litmus test, by some accounts, is yet to be confronted. It is generally conceded that the military services tapped the mother lode of volunteers in the early 1980s, under practically peak demographic and economic conditions. It remains to be seen whether military recruiters can continue their success as several trends, each with adverse implications for military recruitment, converge within the next decade or so.

The declining youth population—the only factor influencing future military recruitment trends that is virtually certain—will have a substantial effect. All other things remaining equal, to maintain an all-volunteer active and reserve force of roughly 3 million under current policies into the 1990s will require that more than one out of every two "qualified and available" young men volunteers for military service, compared with 42 percent in the early 1980s. Whether the military will be able to increase its share of the market is uncertain, with a great deal depending on the state of the economy and on how much the nation is willing to invest in the military payroll. By most economic reckoning, while the number of recruits with high school diplomas can be expected to decline from the unusually high levels of the early 1980s, the armed services can nevertheless expect to attract enough high school graduates to meet congressionally mandated requirements, providing military pay raises keep pace with those in the private sector and economic recovery is not more vigorous than expected.

Should these forecasts prove to be overly optimistic, there are a number of things that could be done to hedge against recruitment shortfalls. For example, the expansion of the role of women, which was scaled back as more men began to volunteer in the early 1980s, could be resumed. Additional civilians, both federal and contract, could be substituted for uniformed personnel in certain occupations. And personnel turnover could be reduced even further by encouraging members of the armed forces to serve for longer periods. On the supply side, military recruiters could attempt to penetrate new markets, such as two-year vocational and technical institutions, which have been virtually untapped by the armed forces. Disagreement exists over the extent to which these changes could be made without undermining military effectiveness, but there is good reason to believe that there is leeway enough, assuming prudent management practices, for the volunteer military to weather the demographics of the next decade.

If, on the other hand, the decline in the youth population is accompanied by a requirement for a substantially larger or more skilled military force, the armed forces could face the prospect of having to draw a sizable proportion of the qualified pool of young men. Under those circumstances, it becomes doubtful that adjusting military pay or tinkering with manpower policies could prevent serious recruitment shortfalls.

These prospects should be taken into account as the nation considers its options for rearming America. Unless the body politic can be counted upon to support peacetime conscription, it would be risky either to expand the size of the armed forces or to develop increasingly complicated weapons systems. If either course, however, is considered vital for security purposes, then the nation's leadership should make these purposes clear and should prepare the American people for the reinstitution of compulsory service. Otherwise, the United States could end up fielding military forces in the 1990s whose effectiveness would depend on a military draft, only to find a citizenry unwilling to support it.